MAKE EACH CLICK COUNT

USING GOOGLE SHOPPING

REVEALING PROFITS & STRATEGIES

ANDY SPLICHAL

www.makeeachclickcount.com

www.trueonlinepresence.com

www.theacademyofinternetmarketing.com

This book is dedicated to my wife,

Claudia, and my children, AJ & Charlotte,

whom continually fuel me with

inspiration and passion.

PREFACE

Google gives advertisers a tremendous opportunity to reach millions of potential buyers and even some training on how to properly use Google if you do the research. However, Google will take practically anyone's money that is willing to spend it with them. In Las Vegas, this is called "dumb money." It is what makes Vegas rich, hell, it is what makes Google rich. But there is a better way.

In Las Vegas - one of their most popular games is blackjack. A relatively simple game, blackjack can be played by anyone over the age of 21. You start with two cards and try to get closer to 21 than the person representing the casino does without going over. If you do that, you win. Easy, right?

Similar to Google, anyone can sit down and start to play as long as they are willing to part with their money. However, some people who wish to play the game first would like to get more educated on rules and strategies to increase their chance of success. There are books on blackjack strategy that, if learned, will increase your odds. There are similar books regarding Google advertising that can increase your odds of success; I should know, I wrote one and hopefully you have read it!

So, what to do, where to start, especially if you are a busy store owner with a thousand things pulling you in a million different directions?

Well, from talking to hundreds of store owners, I have found that there are four specific routes taken and here they are:

Do Absolutely Nothing – This is the easiest option for you. You decide not to sell on Google, maybe electing to advertise on Amazon or a different marketing channel. For store owners, especially online eCommerce store owners, this can be turning your back on the potential for huge number of sales. Plus, if you rely on purely Amazon, you are at Amazon's whim in addition to paying Amazon a steep commission and not even owning the customer.

Do It Yourself – Taking your lumps as you learn. Just like the person who walks into the casino for the first time, you are welcome to jump right in and play. Typically, those players lose, but who knows, we've all heard of beginner's luck, right?

Hire an Agency – Let a SEM agency that you select handle everything for you. Again, maybe they know what they are doing, maybe not. If you are a small to medium sized business, typically large SEM agencies have a great salesperson; however, once you sign on, your account typically goes over to a junior marketer, maybe right out of college. They may very well also take their lumps; however, they get to do it with your money. And, if you don't know the basic best-practices, then how will you even know?

Educate Yourself – At least with basic best-practices in advertising on Google Ads and Google Shopping. Just the like the blackjack newbie, it can be daunting, and it will take some time. However, if you don't learn at least some fundamental best-practices, it can be disastrous for your marketing budget.

By reading *Make Each Click Count Using Google Shopping*, you are taking the 4th and hardest step to educate yourself. I congratulate you for doing so. You have set yourself apart as someone who desires and demands better results from your Google Shopping, and I'm excited to help you get there!

Once you have finished the book, I encourage you to take a trial to www.theacademyofinternetmarketing.com in order to stay in tune with updated changes and the latest strategies and techniques for optimizing your Google Shopping.

TABLE OF CONTENTS

INTRODUCTION

Make Each Click Count Using Google Shopping – Revealing Profits & Strategies is your guide to unlocking profits inside Google Shopping and magnifying those profits using the latest techniques and strategies typically applied by only the top Google Ad agencies.

The fact is that Google Search ads have continued to become more competitive as more and more businesses advertise their products and services using this original Google ad type.

Although opportunities still exist using Google Search ads, most eCommerce advertisers tend to achieve substantially higher profits and generate a substantially higher volume of sales using Google Shopping.

There are two main reasons that overall sales and profitability both are typically higher for companies advertising with Google Shopping ads compared to Google Search ads – how they work and how they are set up.

First – How Google Shopping Ads Work

When Google Shopping ads are displayed, users are shown the product image, price, product name and the name of the merchant before they even click on an ad. In addition, when they do click an ad, users are ALWAYS directed to the product page EVERY time. There is never any confusion on the shopper/user side.

For Google Search ads, on the other hand, even with the best well-written ad copy, some shoppers may be expecting something different when they click on your ad than when they land on your website.

This confusion and surprise will lead to the customer quickly returning to Google (called a bounce). However, even when shoppers bounce, you, the advertiser, are still charged for the visit.

Second – How Google Shopping Ads Are Set Up

For Google Search ads, advertisers go into their Google Ads account, create a list of keywords, create an ad, and typically the ad is live within a few hours.

This simplicity of setting up an ad is the main reason that Google Search, especially, has become more and more competitive.

In order to run a Google Shopping campaign, advertisers first must open and format their Google Merchant Center account. Upload their products into that account and link their Merchant Center account to their Google Ads account.

In order to run a well-optimized Google Shopping campaign, advertisers must then segment their products into different campaigns and adjust their bidding on products, device, location, etc.

Being a bit more complicated is a good thing for the advertisers willing to discover what is available in Google Shopping as being more complicated weeds out the competition that is either too lazy or too distracted to take full advantage of what is available using Google Shopping.

With so many moving pieces to optimize with Google Shopping, it is no wonder that automation such as Google Smart Shopping campaigns are becoming more popular (we will dive into these more in chapter 17 - *Is Using Google Smart Shopping Campaigns Smart for Retailers?*).

For now, know that what is laid out in this book are the current best-practices for quickly increasing your profits and sales using Google Shopping.

Won't This Book Become Outdated?

The short answer is YES.

It is hard to believe that it has been almost five years since I published my first book – *Make Each Click Count – T.O.P. Guide To Success Using Google Ads.*

In the five years since that book was published, the Google interface has changed multiple times. Some of the terminology has changed.

Heck, even the name has changed (Google AdWords is now Google Ads).

However, the strategies and underlying fundamentals for my original book have not changed.

Likewise, with this book, I can promise with absolute certainty that in a year or less (maybe even by the time this book is published) some of the Google Ads interface will have changed.

That is just the nature of Google AdWords (excuse me, I meant to say Google Ads).

However, what won't change are the advanced strategies on how to segment your account and how to use the historical data to optimize your account to predict future success.

What Does This Book Contain?

This book has been divided into 5 main sections.

- Laying The Groundwork – Here Google Shopping is explained including the history, what it has now become and what it looks like.

- Optimizing Google Merchant Center – Properly optimizing Merchant Center with complete data is essential for success using Google Shopping campaigns. This section focuses on the importance of Merchant Center as well as best-practices and common techniques for creating a fully optimized Merchant Center account.

- Basic Optimizations Inside Google Ads – This section covers in detail the strategies and best-practices for optimizing Shopping campaigns inside the Google Ads interface. Discover how to best optimize your campaigns using historical data to predict future success in relations to keywords, adjusting product bids, adjusting mobile bids, adjusting location bids and more.

- Automating Google – The fourth section goes into detail on automated features of Google Shopping including the new Google Smart Shopping campaigns, different automated bid strategies and merchant participating in Google Shopping Actions.

- Advanced Techniques – Written for those wishing to dive even deeper into Google Shopping, this section looks at advanced techniques such as using the Google Ads editor, using supplemental feeds and using positive keywords to control search terms.

How Should You Read This Book?

How to read this book is going to depend on you and what you want to take from the book. Reading the book in order, cover-to-cover, will lead to some great insights in a perspective you have never thought about – even for the most experienced advertiser – and provide a full look at advanced techniques and strategies.

For the advertiser just starting with Google Shopping, this book will lead them through a journey from inception to completion with a step-by-step guide to create and maintain successful Google Shopping campaigns.

If you are pressed for time, start reading the chapter that details where you currently need help in your account. However, make sure you return to read the full book!

Why Did I Write This Book?

My name is Andy Splichal, and I have been managing Google Ads campaigns for almost twenty years! Since 2001, I've managed hundreds of thousands of dollars for my clients.

Since 2014, I have managed Google Ads for private clients through True Online Presence, where I'm the founder and CEO.

True Online Presence is a partnered Google Ads agency that continually strives to provide profits through best-practices and cutting-edge proprietary strategies for our private clients using Search, Shopping and Display ads.

Since publishing my first book in 2015 – *Make Each Click Count – T.O.P. Guide To Success Using Google Shopping,* the opportunity for profitability has shifted to Google Shopping ad types.

And although the original book included a section on Google Shopping, there was not enough specific step-by-step detail for someone to create a successful Shopping campaign TODAY.

That is why I released this book, to demonstrate how we are optimizing Shopping accounts with great success for our private clients and invite those willing to put in the work to not only read this book, but to apply the techniques taught in order to enjoy the same level of success!

I hope you enjoy the book.

Andy Splichal

A BONUS CHAPTER
BEFORE WE BEGIN

It's Deja Vu All Over Again With
Free Google Shopping

You perhaps read in the introduction of the book where I addressed the question, won't this book become outdated?

I answered with an absolute YES, well at least kind of yes.

Google continues to update their advertising interface as well as how they display ads inside Google and within Google network.

So yes, in the fact that the screenshots in this book will no doubt become outdated over time.

But no, the strategies and underlying fundamentals will not soon become outdated and if properly executed will continue to grow your sales and profitability for years to come.

With that said, the day after I originally sent the book to Amazon's printing department, Google announced a change large enough for me to temporarily put the printing on hold until I could add this bonus chapter addressing the change.

What was the major announcement?

Google announced that after eight years they would again start listing free organic Shopping ads within Google's Shopping.

For retailers, being able to show products for free means that any retailer could now have their products showing within the Google Shopping tab as part of the **surfaces across Google** program.

For shoppers using Google Shopping this change will translate into more variety when shopping and more merchants and more products from which to shop.

Reasons For Offering Free Listings

Google provided the reason they are once again making Google free is to help businesses negatively impacted during the COVID-19 pandemic.

It is true that by allowing merchants to list products at no charge within the surfaces across Google program, they are allowing millions of merchants and shoppers to connect without taking Google's usual cut.

It is also true that Google has vowed to give small and medium sized businesses $340 million in ad credits that advertisers will be able to use between when they are issued and by the end of 2020.

However, the free shopping listings is not an idea that just materialized. The idea has been in the works from Google to combat Amazon in the fight for market share of online shopping.

By allowing more advertisers to list their products, Google will be able to give their shoppers a better shopping experience by allowing for more selection. And although not originally altruistically motivated, one should applaud Google for speeding up the release of the program as well as the ad credits for eligible small businesses.

What Does It Mean For Existing Advertisers?

It is important to note that free product listings are only going to be eligible to appear within the Google Shopping tab. The prime real estate on the main search results page as well as the top and bottom of the Shopping tab page will still be reserved for paid ads with no change to how they are currently structured.

Therefore, by making sure that you are opted into showing inside **surfaces across Google** program, paying advertisers should see some additional free traffic. This free traffic will be a nice bonus to existing advertising, but it should not be expected to replace the volume of traffic being generated through paid ads.

Free product ads should start automatically being displayed inside the Google Shopping tab, but to make sure products are in fact displaying advertisers will want to ensure Google has opted them into the program.

To confirm opt in, advertisers will want to visit their Merchant Center account. Once there, they will need to navigate to "Growth" in the left-hand menu and select "Manage programs". Within Manage programs, advertisers will be able to determine if the "surfaces across Google" program card is already showing 'Active'.

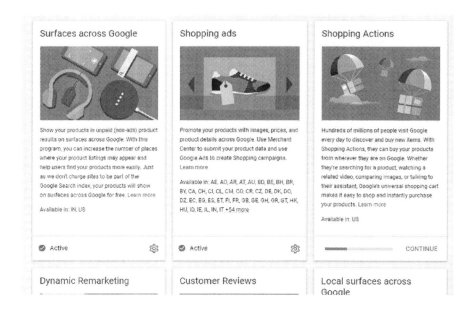

Note, that this account has surfaces across Google as active. This confirms that products are eligible to appear for free in the Google Shopping tab.

You can also now view inside your Merchant Center dashboard the number of free traffic visits alongside the paid traffic visits. Although it is only a couple of days into the program, the image below shows the number of free traffic visits for this account approximately 2% of the daily paid traffic.

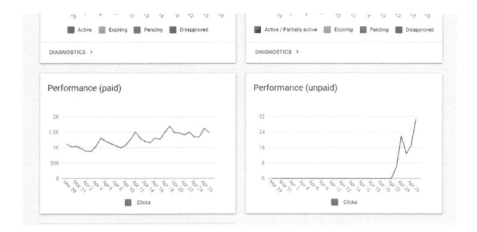

Like I said earlier, advertisers should not expect the amount of free traffic to replace the volume of current paid traffic!

Instead, paid advertisers would be wise to think of the additional free traffic as a nice supplement.

What Does It Mean For Those Not Previously Advertising With Google Shopping?

For those who had not currently been advertising with Google Shopping, they will now be able have their products listed within the surfaces across Google program at no charge.

However, before they are eligible to have their products display, a merchant will need to first open a Google Merchant Center account and then upload their products into Google Merchant Center.

The most popular way to upload products is through a data feed. Many e-commerce platforms such as Shopify and Big Commerce have free downloads that can be used.

However, as we discussed several times already in this book, you really get what you pay for when using these free services. Even if a company wants to take advantage of the free Google traffic only, it would be well advised to shell out a couple of bucks per month to use a 3rd party data optimization company.

It also is important to note for anyone expecting a ton of free traffic from this change that the products opted into the free surfaced across Google will not get priority placement. Priority placement will still be reserved for paid ads.

With that said, there will absolutely be opportunity to receive free traffic through Google Shopping that was not available before the announcement. With some work, new advertisers can take advantage of this opportunity from Google and receive some free traffic at absolutely no charge.

Final Word

This change for Google to again start showing free listings appears to be a win-win situation.

First, for Google, it gives them more products to display to their shoppers providing a better shopping experience.

Second, for paying advertisers, they are not losing any of the priority placements inside Google Shopping. Therefore, they are not losing any optimization work that may have been done optimizing their custom labels for product ads and bidding inside the Google Ads interface.

In addition, paid advertisers also are going to pick up some free incremental traffic to help supplement their paid Google Shopping efforts.

Third, for new advertisers not currently using Google Shopping, this is an opportunity to test Google Shopping absolutely free. I consistently find Google Shopping to have one of the best ROIs available for e-commerce retailers and now it is available on a limited basis to all retailers at no charge.

Overall, this is a change from Google where I can't see anyone who will not benefit and there is plenty of room to be excited whether you are a paid advertisers, want to show your products for free or just want more options when shopping online.

And now that we have gotten the bonus chapter added, let's get on with the rest of the book!

SECTION 1

Laying The Groundwork

CHAPTER 1

Google Shopping – What It Is, How It Has Changed

Google Shopping is by far the largest Comparison Shopping Engine aka CSE on the Internet. CSEs are used exclusively by eCommerce advertisers, not professional services advertisers. This is because Comparison Shopping Engines allow customers to compare the same product or type of products from multiple stores simultaneously.

Although there are other Comparison Shopping Engines, many of which have gone by the wayside, Google Shopping has captured the vast majority of the market share.

Companies such as PriceGrabber, Nextag, BizRate, Shopzilla, Pronto and Shopping.com have been outpaced and left behind by Google and the opportunities that Google brings to its advertisers.

In order to have your products eligible to appear inside the Google Shopping platform, advertisers must first open a Google Merchant Center account and then upload their products into the Merchant Center platform.

Typically for retailers with a substantial number of products, a data feed is formatted in either a csv or txt format. Although there are other ways, including API connections, most advertisers use the formatted feed method to upload their products.

The ability for merchants to upload their products to Google Merchant Center has given rise to quite a few data optimization companies. Some will also manage your feed (we can get into that later), but for the most part, their services exist to make an advertiser's life easier when it comes to getting their products approved and ready to advertise on the Google Shopping platform.

Before we go any further, let's take a quick look at the history of how Google Shopping came to dominate the comparison shopping space.

Google Shopping was a free service until October 2012 called Froogle. In October 2012, Google went to a cost per click model similar to Google text ads where advertisers would pay each time one of their product ads was clicked. Although it was free to list prior to October 2012, the reporting abilities and customer support from Google was almost non-existent.

When Google changed to a CPC model, they made their Google Shopping system much more user friendly, allowing advertisers to manage their Shopping campaign inside their Google Ads console, allowing different bidding options and adding full customer support. Google has also made Google Shopping more prominent in how they display it to their users.

What Google Shopping Looks Like

There have been many variations over the years of where Google Shopping ads appear on Google as Google continues to experiment with the best-placement for these high performing ads.

Currently, Google Shopping ads are seen either in an expandable carousel at the top of the page above both text ads and organic placements or in a limited view on the right side, which typically occurs for branded term searches.

To illustrate the difference, let's look at search results for 'baseball gloves' vs. 'Wilson baseball gloves'

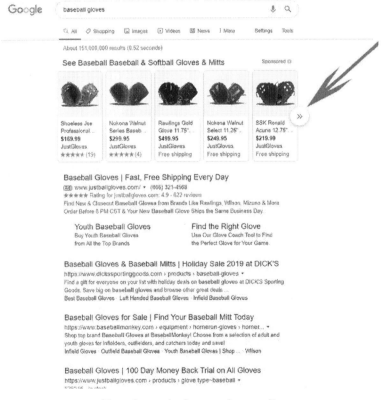

Non-branded search results

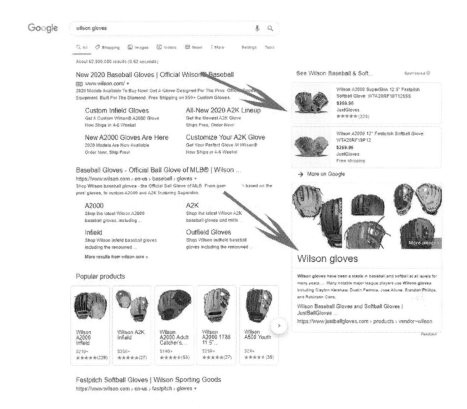

Branded search results

As you can see, the generic search results for 'baseball gloves' yields 5 Shopping ads located above the search ads and the organic listings. In this case, JustGloves has every shopping listing shown as well as the Search Text ad. What a great job they are doing with their Google marketing!

If you click on the arrow, more results for Shopping ads are shown. In addition, users can find more Shopping ads inside the 'Shopping' tab where shoppers can compare the same item from multiple sellers on the same listing. Shoppers are also able to sort their searches by price, brand and other criteria such as fielding position in this example.

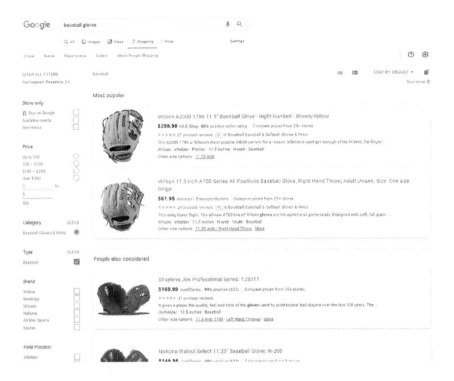

For branded searches such as 'Wilson gloves' you can see in the image above that Shopping ads are not shown on top. Instead, there is a Search text ad. The Shopping ads, again for JustGloves, are shown on the right side of the organic results along with information about the searched brand.

How To Implement Google Shopping

For advertisers to participate in Google Shopping, they must have an active Google Ads account as well as a Google Merchant Center account with approved products.

The Google Merchant Center account is where advertisers upload their products, typically through a data feed. This data feed must contain their current product listing that they wish to make eligible for inclusion within the Google shopping database. To open a Google Merchant Center account, visit https://www.google.com/merchants/.

The Google Ads account is where advertisers can create a Shopping campaign and where merchants will link their Shopping campaign in order to control bids and their Shopping ads placement.

It sounds much more complicated than it is. Once an advertiser opens a Google Merchant Center account and uploads a feed and verifies that they own the website in Merchant Center, they can quickly link to their Ads account simply by sending an invitation from Merchant Center to their ads account.

Easy, right?

The part that is a little more involved is setting up the csv file for the Google merchant feed. Google supports a variety of different attributes for each product. Attributes currently supported include: id, title, description, Google merchant category, product type, link, mobile link, image link, additional image link, condition, availability, availability date, price, sale price, brand, gtin, mpn, identifier exists, gender, age group, size type, color, size, material, pattern, shipping, shipping weight, excluded destination, expiration date, product applicability, promotion id, product review average, product review count and five custom labels.

The purpose of so many attributes is to allow Google to serve the most refined results to their users performing Google searches. It may sound a bit overwhelming, but the good news is that there are many services that help merchants convert their products into the correct formats that are accepted by Google.

However, most of these services do not work right out of the box and may need some customization in order to correctly populate as many fields as possible.

This is where using a 3rd party Google data optimization company is extremely helpful, especially for merchants with a large number of product offerings.

It is in the best-interest of advertisers to populate as many of these fields as are relevant to their product listings. Populating fields correctly will help advertisers' products appear more often and appear more relevant to searches performed. It will also allow advertisers' products to be accurately grouped with other merchants retailing the same product which will allow for your product ad in a Google Shopping campaign to be displayed.

Therefore, when selecting a feed provider, double-check that the provider has the capabilities to both deliver Google a correctly formatted feed as well as the ability to convert existing data from your website to the appropriate Google field attributes.

Final Word

Google Shopping generally delivers a better ROI (return on investment) and generally higher conversion rates compared to using straight text ads. This is due to how they appear. Google Shopping ads show customers an image of an item along with the price. In contrast, Google text ads provide only a text description. Even the most detailed description may not convey what is in the customer's mind, and therefore, the customer may click on an ad (costing the advertiser money) and not be taken to the product or products that they expected, thus leaving.

Advertisers not using Google Shopping ads will not appear in the Google Shopping results, either in the Shopping carousel or withing the Shopping section of Google.

As simple as that sounds, I've spoken to retailers before who have said to me, "Hey Andy, I'm advertising on Google, why are my products not being shown under Google Shopping?"

And the answer is: only products in the Google Shopping database as submitted to Google Merchant Center are eligible to show on Google Shopping, and an advertiser needs to set up their products using the processes described above in order for their products to be eligible to appear.

Once an advertiser has their products appearing in Google Shopping, the work has just begun. Just like search campaigns, a Google Shopping campaign must be fully optimized in order to produce the best possible results and the 'biggest bang for the buck'.

If you are an eCommerce merchant, then selling your products inside Google Shopping is an absolute must as a strategy to substantially grow your online sales.

CHAPTER 2

There Can Be No Google Shopping Without A Google Merchant Account

For many eCommerce merchants, Google Shopping is essential to their online sales strategy and new customer acquisition. With Google search ads becoming ever more expensive, many retailers are finding their best ROI opportunities with the implementation of properly optimized Google Shopping ads.

In order to fully optimize, advertisers adjust their Google Shopping product bids and segment their products within the Google Ads interface. For best-practices and effective strategies on optimizing Google Shopping within the Google Ads interface, we will go into full detail in upcoming chapters.

However, before products are eligible to appear in Google Shopping, products must first become eligible to appear. For products to become eligible to appear, they must be properly formatted and approved inside a Google Merchant Center Account.

In addition, for advertisers wishing to advertise their products using Google's Shopping Actions Program, creating a Merchant Center account is also required for participation.

The Basics – Google's Merchant Center

A Google Merchant Center Account is an account that Google requires merchants to open before they can have their products eligible to list within Google Shopping or Shopping Actions. It is where merchants upload their full product data containing information on the products they wish to advertise within Google Shopping network.

In order to get started, new advertisers need to create an account by visiting www.google.com/retail/solutions/merchant-center/ and clicking on the 'Get Started' button. When creating a new account, advertisers will be required to supply the name of their store, Website URL and whether the website contains content as defined by Google.

Add a new account

Name of your store ⑦

Enter a value

Your website (optional)

Website URL

☐ My site contains adult products as defined by Google's policy. Learn more

CANCEL   SAVE

Next, an advertiser will need to verify and claim the URL for the account they create.

In order to claim a website, owners have the options of adding some HTML code to their metatags, using information in their Google Analytics tags or information contained in their Google Tag Manager. Any of the methods will work, and therefore, it is left to the discretion of individual advertisers to select which method they prefer.

Once the tags are implemented, advertisers can quickly determine whether the process of claiming and verifying worked, and if successful, the site will change status to being verified and claimed.

In addition, an advertiser can determine if their account has been successfully claimed and verified at any time by clicking on the 'Account Settings' link under the Settings link (wrench icon) in the top menu.

Once an advertiser has claimed and verified their account, they will have full functionality throughout the account. However, to properly manage their Google Merchant Center Account, advertisers will need to understand the layout of where different options and settings are located.

Exploring Google's Merchant Center Layout

Each Merchant Center account uses a left-hand menu that includes the following options: Overview, Orders (if Shopping Actions is enabled), Products, Performance (if Shopping Actions is enabled), Marketing and Growth.

Overview

The overview is a dashboard containing a quick snapshot of the account. Although, for new merchants the dashboard will be blank, for existing merchants the dashboard becomes an important snapshot into the health of the account.

For advertisers with account history, the dashboard will display a summary overview of their products including a graph displaying active products, expiring products, products awaiting review and disapproved products for Surfaces across Google, Shopping Ads and Shopping Actions (if enabled).

In addition, the dashboard will show a graph displaying the account's paid click history as well as Google announcements.

Orders

This link will only appear for merchants who have been approved to have their products appear within Google's Shopping Actions.

Within the orders section, merchants will find orders from Google Shopping Actions that are Pending, Pending Delivery and All Orders (history). The Orders link also contains historical return data, again for Google Shopping Action orders only.

Products

The Products link is going to be the most used of the links within the left-hand navigation. Within the Product link, merchants can access 'Diagnostics', 'All Products' and 'Feeds'.

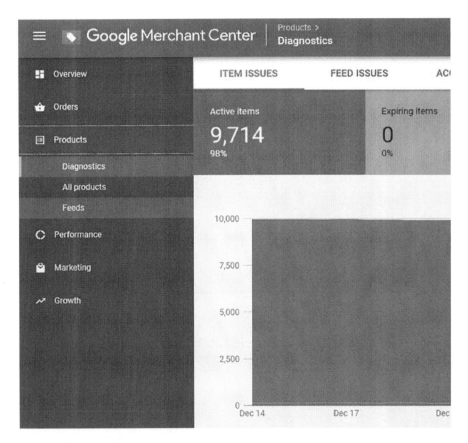

Diagnostics – This section shows advertisers any potential issues with products within their submitted data. Diagnostic information can be viewed based on destination (dynamic remarketing, shopping actions, shopping ads or surfaces across Google); although shopping ads is the default view. In addition, the diagnostics data can be viewed by the Country ads are served as well as by specific Feed.

Reviewing the Merchant Center's diagnostics is essential in determining which products are eligible for display in Google Shopping and/or Shopping Actions. These insights are NOT available in the Google Ads interface and is one reason that reviewing the Merchant Center Account on a regular basis is highly recommended.

Diagnostics will provide the number of items currently disapproved, awaiting review, expiring and active. In addition, the diagnostics link contains information on the status of the account, feeds and individual items. If there are issues present in any of these areas, diagnostics will also generate links helpful for fixing listed issues as well as provide examples of items with current issues and the ability to download all items affected by listed errors.

In this account example, the diagnostics view contains links to affected items with errors in the feed. By clicking on the 'View samples' link, an advertiser can determine how many of their products are currently being affected and by which issues. Note that not all listed issues will keep products from being eligible for display; however, next to the issue, Google will list if the error causes products to be disapproved or if this issue is a warning.

All products – The 'All products' link allows advertisers to view all of their products. They can view details on individual products by clicking on the title.

In addition, advertisers can filter and search for specific data based on Title, ID, Price, Clicks, Condition, Availability, Status, Channel, Country or Language.

The 'All products' link is essential to use when confirming whether a specific product is listed and what attributes for specific products have been indexed into Google's database. This can be done through this view quickly without the need to open and review the actual data feed.

Feeds

Within the feeds link, advertisers can review current feeds as well as create and schedule new feeds. Feed types are categorized into Primary Feeds and Supplemental Feeds.

Primary feeds are used by Google Merchant Center to upload product data via text (txt) files, XML (.xml) files, Google Sheets or the Google Center API.

Supplemental feeds are used by Merchant Center as a secondary data source to provide additional attributes to your primary feeds or to provide additional data to be used within Feed Rules.

Once a data feed has been successfully uploaded, approved products are eligible to appear within the Google Shopping network for 30 days. So, at the absolute minimum, merchants will need to re-upload their data monthly. However, typically for eCommerce merchants where their product information changes, in order to stay current with data, products will require more regular uploads, typically daily or at least weekly.

The process of uploading a new data feed is the easy part of getting items approved in Google's Shopping network. More involved is creation of the actual feed. Google currently supports 46 different attributes, and although not all attributes are required, it is recommended that advertisers populate as many fields as possible that are relevant for their products.

Current supported attributes include: link, title, description, price, sale_price, sale_price_effective_date, mobile_link, image_link, id, brand, condition, manufacturer, mpn, gtin, identifier_exists, shipping_weight, product_type, shipping, multipack, is_bundle, adwords_grouping, adwords_labels, excluded_destination, expiration_date, promotion_id, availability, availability_date, google_product_category, color, size, size_type, size_system, material, pattern, additional_image_link, age_group, gender, adult, item_group, custom_label_0, custom_label_1, custom_label_2, custom_label_3, custom_label_4, shipping_height, shipping_width, shipping_length and cost_of_goods_sold.

Don't worry, there are 3rd party data optimization companies that work with advertisers for a nominal fee to set-up regular data feed uploads and populate different fields based on information currently contained within eCommerce websites.

Performance
The performance link will appear for retailers who have been approved to sell products through Google's Shopping Actions program.

The performance view allows advertisers to keep track of retailer standards to make sure they are meeting Google Shopping Actions performance standards as well as keep track of Shopping Actions promotions.

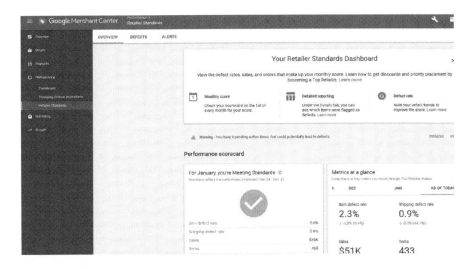

Note, advertisers participating in Shopping Actions that meet top retailer status will have their items shown more often in Shopping Actions while those who consistently fall below standards may find their products eventually suspended from appearing within Google Shopping Actions.

Marketing

The marketing link contains Promotions and Product reviews. Both promotions and product reviews are free to use; however, you will need to request that they are enabled from the Google Shopping team before you see them in your Google Merchant Center console.

Promotions allow advertisers to stand apart from their competition who sell the same or similar products. A strategic way to bring added emphasis to product listings, review chapter 7 *Enhancing Google Shopping Using Promotions* for details on creating and implementing promotions within Google Merchant Center.

For advertisers who collect product reviews, this feature allows their product ratings and reviews to be shown directly on their Google Shopping listing. Note, for a merchant to qualify to use product reviews, they must have a minimum of 50 product reviews gathered within the last 12 months. In order to remain eligible, merchants will need to update their product reviews at least once per month through a data upload into their Google Merchant Center account.

Growth

The Growth link contains suggestions from Google to grow your account and includes Opportunities, Market insights, Shopping Actions insights (if approved) and Manage programs.

Opportunities – Lists where there may be potential opportunities to increase your traffic using Google Shopping. Examples of opportunities include fixing errors on historically high traffic Shopping ads.

Marketing insights – This view shows popular products on Google that you're not currently advertising. In the "Personalized" view, the products are selected based on how similar they are to your most popular products and ranked based on how many clicks an ad for that product is likely to receive. Along with the products, you'll also see prices for those products from other retailers.

The "Personalized" tab shows you products that you might want to advertise based on your current products, ranked by how many clicks an ad for that product would receive. These products are related to what you're currently advertising.

Shopping Actions insights (for merchants who have been accepted into Shopping actions) – This view helps advertisers understand your price competitiveness on Shopping Actions and how you can win the buy-box. This view allows advertisers to filter by specific products in order to gain insight into which products they are winning buy box with Google Shopping Actions.

Manage programs – This view allows advertisers to easily manage which available features are enabled within their Merchant Center account. Currently available programs include Surfaces across Google, Shopping ads, Shopping Actions, Dynamic Remarketing, Customer Reviews, Local inventory ads, Merchant Promotions and Product Ratings.

Settings

The final option located (as a Wrench icon) in the upper menu is Settings.

📇 TOOLS

Shipping and returns

Sales tax

Business information

Payments

Shopping ads setup

Shopping Actions setup

Customer Reviews setup

Surfaces across Google

🗂 SETTINGS

Content API

Account settings

Account access

Preferences

Linked accounts

Automatic improvements

SFTP / FTP / GCS

Settings are broken into two subcategories – Tools and Settings.

Tools consists of all the settings a merchant needs to complete in order to have their account approved. These include Shipping and Returns, Sales tax, Business information, Payments, Shopping ads setup, Shopping Actions setup (if approved), Customer Reviews setup and Surfaces Across Google.

> Shipping and Returns – where a merchant formats their shipping and return information. Information submitted here needs to fully match what is listed on the website.

Sales tax – where a merchant formats where and at what rates they collect sales tax on orders.

Business information – The business display name along with address and customer service contact information.

Payments (merchants with Shopping Actions) – payment information of where Google will send settled money received from orders placed using Google Shopping actions.

Shopping ads setup – Information regarding participation in Google Shopping ads including notices, status and product/business information.

Shopping Actions setup (merchants with Shopping Actions) – Information regarding participation in Shopping Actions including notices, status and product/business information.

Customer reviews setup – Data about the number of customers who have opted in and completed Google's Customer Review surveys.

Surfaces across Google - Information regarding participation in Surfaces across Google including notices, status and product/business information.

The Settings subcategory includes Content API, Account settings, Account access, Preferences, Linked accounts, Automatic improvements and SFTP, FTP, GCS.

Content API – Historical data for the account regarding successful and failed API calls. This is where you can create a Google API Key for your Google Merchant Center account.

Account Settings – This includes time zone and language as well as account status and where you can close your account.

Account Access – Allows merchants to grant permissions to different users to whom they wish to allow access to their Merchant Center account.

Preferences – Allows merchants to adjust access levels for various users and control levels of automatic notifications from Google.

Linked accounts – Allows you to link your Merchant Center Account to your Google Ads account. This must be done prior to being able to serve product ads within Google.

Automatic improvements – Allows merchants to enable automatic item updates for price, availability and both.

SFTP, FTP, GCS – Access to SFTP, FTP and GCS settings in order to be able to upload products directly into your Merchant Center account based on these available delivery methods.

Final Word

Although once a merchant has set up their Google Merchant Center Account and has their product data automatically and successfully updating, it can be tempting to forget about the Merchant Center and fully concentrate efforts on optimizing listings exclusively within the Google Ads interface.

Optimizing listings and categories within the Google Ads interface is essential to the success of Google Shopping Campaigns. However, equally important is the regular monitoring of the Google Merchant Center Account.

For it is only within the Google Merchant Center Account that advertisers can view issues related to their product data that may prevent items from being eligible to display; learn insights regarding other advertisers and configure account information such as shipping, tax and contact information.

For these reasons, without constantly monitoring your Google Merchant Center Account, it will not be possible to fully optimize your Google Shopping listings.

CHAPTER 3

Linking Merchant Account to the Google Ads Interface

Once you have created your Google Merchant Center account, you must link the Merchant Center account to your Google Ads account before you can begin running Google Shopping campaigns.

Google needs to verify that you have access to both accounts as well as a way to match specific products in Merchant Center with a particular Google Ads account.

Linking is a quick step that takes only a few minutes, but many times, those new to Google Shopping will forget this step and wonder why they cannot access their products when creating their first Google Shopping campaign.

How To Link From Merchant Center

1. Sign into your Google Merchant Center Account.

2. Click on the Settings (Wrench) icon in the top menu and select 'Linked accounts'.

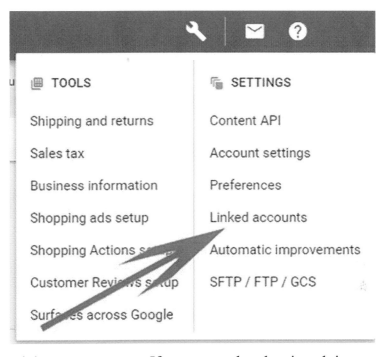

3. Link your account. If you are already signed into your Google Ads account, Google will pre-populate your Google Ads Customer ID. If you do not see the customer ID or need to link to a different account, click on the Link account and enter the customer ID as prompted.

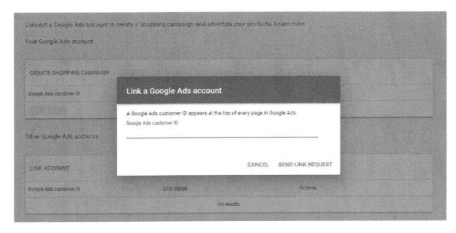

4. Once you send a link request, you will need to log in to your Google Ads Account.

5. Once inside your Google Ads Account, click on the Tools & Settings (Wrench Icon) in the top menu and select 'Linked Accounts'. By clicking linked accounts, you will be able to view all of the possible Google programs that you can link to your Google Ads Account. For our purpose, we will want to scroll down to Google Merchant Center and click on the DETAILS link.

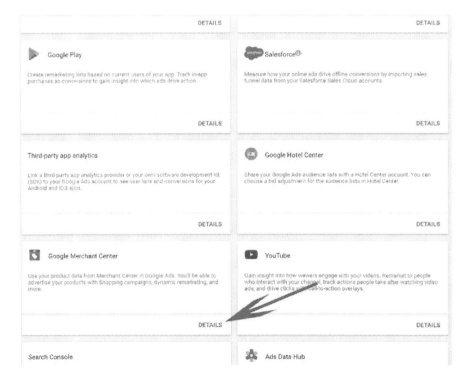

6. Once you click on the DETAILS link for Google Merchant Center, you will be able to view the pending request to link

to your Google Ads account as well as existing Merchant Center Accounts that have been previously linked. In order to accept a request, simply click the VIEW DETAILS link under Actions and Approve the request.

You've got one pending request from Merchant Center. Approve or reject below. Learn more		
Account ↑	Status	Actions
Details	Pending	VIEW DETAILS
TOP_Test www.testaccount.com	Linked	UNLINK

That is it. You should now have your Merchant Center account linked to your Google Ads account and will be ready to begin advertising using Google Shopping campaigns.

Note, in order to be able to link accounts, you must have an 'Admin' role in Merchant Center and have 'Administrative Access' in order to approve Merchant Center linking request inside of Google Ads.

Final Word

The final step is preparing to launch your first Google Shopping campaign; linking to your Google Ads account is a relatively quick and easy step.

Once you have the account properly linked, make sure you have verified and claimed your website inside of Merchant Center, completed your shipping and tax settings and uploaded your products.

If everything has been properly configured, after you link your accounts, you will now be ready to launch your first Google Shopping campaign.

CHAPTER 4

Measuring Conversions – Implementing Proper Tracking

A few weeks before completing this book, I conducted a welcome call with a customer taking a trial to my online training membership - The Academy of Internet Marketing. While on the welcome call, she asked the question, "How can she tell where her conversions are coming from?"

Although it may seem basic to those online marketers with experience, for advertisers just starting out, being able to determine how conversions are generated is a vital question that needs to be addressed. After all, what gets measured gets improved, and if you can't measure it, well then, how can you improve it?

Options for Tracking Conversions

To track sales or other events, advertisers first must add a small bit of tracking code to their website often referred to as snippet. This snippet of unique JavaScript code is automatically created by each marketing channel and allows the advertiser to track users arriving to their website along with actions that a user takes and then integrate the action into their reporting.

This process of adding code works the same way (of course with a different code) whether it is Google, Bing, Facebook or an array of other paid and organic marketing channels.

For sales coming from Google Ads, there are several ways to track conversions along with several options for what type of conversions to track. With the use of a Google Ads code snippet, advertisers are able to track sales and other actions on their website; track app install and other actions on their apps; track calls from your ads or your website or advertisers can import conversions from other systems including Google Analytics.

In addition, advertisers also have the option of tracking conversions through Google Analytics by adding a global site tag or through the use of Google's tag manager.

Tracking Conversions Using Google Ads

The most common conversion to track for eCommerce stores is the purchase of an item. In order to start tracking conversions, there are two main pieces.

First, create the conversion action.

Second, add the conversion tracking tag to your website.

Creating The Conversion Action

1. Log in to your Google Ads Account.

2. In the upper right corner, click the tools icon 🔧, and under "Measurement," select Conversions.

3. Select the plus button ➕.

4. Select Website.

5. Next, you need to select the action you wish to track. If you want to track conversions, you will select Purchase.

6. Then, you will want to enter the conversion name. I recommend giving it a recognizable name such as 'website sale' or 'website purchase'.

7. You will then be asked to select the "Value" of the conversion. Here you have 3 options:

    *   Use the same value for each conversion. Enter the amount each conversion is worth to your business.

    *   Use different values for each conversion. Use this option if, for example, you're tracking purchases of products with different prices. Later, when you add your conversion tracking tag, you'll need to customize your tag to work to track specific values.

    *   Don't use a value.

8. The next option is how you want to count conversions. Here you have two more options:

- One. This setting is recommended for leads, such as a sign-up form on your website, when only one conversion per ad click likely adds value for your business (such as an opt-in or lead).

- Every. This setting is recommended for sales, when every conversion likely adds value for your business.

9. Then you need to select conversion window. This determines how long the system will track conversions after an ad interaction from the drop-down. The window can be 1 to 90 days. The industry norm is 30 days.

10. Click View-through conversion window. Select how long to track view-through conversions from the drop-down. The window can be 1 to 30 days. The default on this option is 1 day. This is going to be used for remarketing. I typically leave this setting at 1 day.

11. Then, you need to select whether you want to include this as a conversion in your reporting. Typically, this option is set to Yes unless you are setting up a conversion that you don't want to count in your reporting, which would generally NOT be the case for tracking an online purchase.

12. Finally, you will need to select the attribution model.

- Last click: Gives all credit for the conversion to the last-clicked ad and corresponding keyword. When using the last click model, you might notice a slight time lag between what's reported in the "Conversions (current model)" column and the "Conversions" column for recent time periods. This lag eventually corrects itself.

- First click: Gives all credit for the conversion to the first-clicked ad and corresponding keyword.

- Linear: Distributes the credit for the conversion equally across all clicks on the path.

- Time decay: Gives more credit to clicks that happened closer in time to the conversion. Credit is distributed using a 7-day half-life. In other words, a click 8 days before a conversion gets half as much credit as a click 1 day before a conversion.

- Position-based: Gives 40% of credit to both the first- and last-clicked ads and corresponding keyword, with the remaining 20% spread out across the other clicks on the path.

- Data-driven: Distributes credit for the conversion based on past data for this conversion action (this is only available to accounts with enough data.)

Note, over the last year, I have been transitioning my private clients to the Position-based attribution option as it seems to provide the clearest picture of how a sale occurs.

13. Click Create and continue.

You'll now see a screen that shows you've created your conversion action. Follow the instructions in the next section to set up your tag.

Adding Conversion Tracking Tags

Once you have your conversion goal configured, you need to add two bits of code to your website for Google Ads to be able to track when a conversion occurs.

The first piece of code (the global site tag) needs to be placed on every page of your website, within the header of your website between the <head> and the </head> tags. The global site tag works to add visitors to your "all visitors" remarketing list, if configured, and will set a new cookie on your domain that will store information about the ad click that brought a visitor to your website.

The event snippet code needs to be placed on the page that counts as your conversion, typically the thank you/confirmation page for eCommerce retailers.

If you set up more than one conversion action for your website, such as transaction and lead, each conversion action will need its own event snippet code added.

For the global site tag, you will have three options on the code you install based on whether this is the first type of Google code you have installed or you've already installed a global site tag from Analytics or if you are using Google Tag Manager.

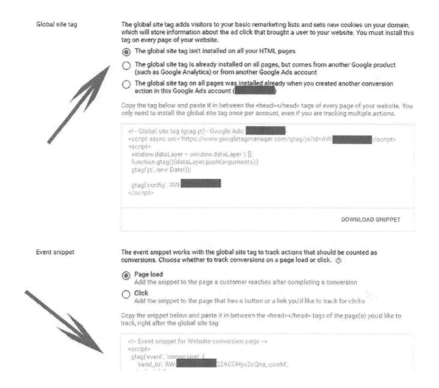

Once you have the appropriate codes, you will need to determine how to add to your website header and confirmation page. Depending on what platform your website it built, the directions will vary. A direct search such as 'adding google tracking tags to Shopify' or 'how to add Google Ads tracking to Big Commerce' will bring up links to detailed directions of how to add the code to your specific website platform.

Tracking Conversions Using Google Analytics

While Google Ads tracking code gives advertisers the ability to track conversions from traffic generated from Google Ads, by using

Google Analytics, advertisers can track conversions from all traffic sources.

Assuming you already have an active Google Analytics account, here are the instructions for starting to track conversions for an eCommerce website:

1. Log in to your Google Analytics account.

2. Click Admin (lower left corner).

3. Select your account from the menu in the *ACCOUNT* column.

4. Select a property from the menu in the *PROPERTY* column.

5. Under *PROPERTY*, click Tracking Info > Tracking Code.

Like Google Ads tracking code, you will have the option for either adding the global site tag or using Google Tag Manager. If you already have the Global Site Tag on your page from Google Ads, then you need to just add the 'config' line of code.

Once you've added the code, you will need to enable your eCommerce settings.

1. Log in to your Google Analytics account.

2. Click Admin (lower left corner).

3. In the *VIEW* column, click Ecommerce Settings.

4. Set *Enable Ecommerce* to ON.

5. Click Save.

These settings should allow you to start the basics of tracking for conversions.

The last step for those who use a 3rd party checkout system such as PayPal, Google Pay or Apple Pay is to add those domains to the Referral Exclusion List. In order to use the 'Referral Exclusion List' navigate under *PROPERTY* > Tracking Info. Advertisers will want to add all URLs and variations to 3rd party checkouts they are using such as 'paypal.com', 'applepay.com', etc.

A quick side note for advertisers that setup tracking conversions in both Google Ads and Google Analytics.

Where you can select the attribution model in Google Ads (last click, first click, linear, time decay, position based or data-driven), Google Analytics uses last non-direct click attribution model for non-multi-channel funnel reports and last click model for multi-channel funnel reports.

This difference in attribution will create slight differences in reporting between the two systems.

Linking Google Ads & Google Analytics

Once you have Google Ads and Google Analytics tracking both properly configured you will want to make sure you link these accounts.

1. Open Google Analytics.

2. Click Admin and choose which account and property you'd like to manage.

3. Under property, click **Google Ads** linking.

4. Click + New Link Group.

5. Select the accounts you want to link.

6. Enter your Link Group Title.

7. Switch on all sites where you want **Google Ads** data.

8. Click link accounts.

By linking your Google Ads and Analytics accounts, you will be able to see Google Ads conversions under Acquisition inside the Analytics dashboard.

Linking your accounts also gives you the ability to import goals that are created inside Analytics into your Google Ads account (a more advanced technique). For now, your account should be all configured with tracking eCommerce conversions.

Final Word

For eCommerce companies it is critical to know exactly where sales are being generated and at exactly what advertising costs. Google gives advertisers the ability to track sales generated from Google Ads as well as through other marketing channels through the proper use of Google Analytics absolutely free.

Properly installing your tracking, however, is just the beginning. Advertisers will need to keep a close watch on their conversions to make sure there are no sudden declines or spikes on any marketing channels and use Google Ads tracking and the data gathered in order to optimize ads.

For my private clients, I am constantly using Google's conversion tracking when working to fully optimize their product and search ads in order to generate maximum profitability.

SECTION 2

Optimizing Google Merchant Center

We moved into our current home in 2013 when my son was four-years old. Towering in the middle of the backyard is a 100-year old avocado tree stretching about 25 feet tall with a base about three and half feet around.

The tree was one of the things that drew my wife and I to the house, but for different reasons. My wife loves avocados.

For me it brought back some childhood memories of the treehouse my neighbors had when I was growing up and how I had always wished I had a treehouse.

In fact, at the time one of the shows that my four-year old son and I would watch religiously was *Treehouse Masters* on Animal Planet, so yes, I was looking at that avocado tree in the yard in a much different way than my wife.

When summertime rolled around, I was able to convince my wife to sign-off on the treehouse construction (as long as the tree would not be harmed) and 'mission treehouse' was under way.

Fortunately, one of my friends was an unemployed contractor who also had an affinity for treehouses. In early June, we set to the project with an initial $1K budget in mind and a general idea of what we wanted.

Every Saturday, we worked. Every Sunday, we worked. During the week every other evening, I would stain and sand boards at ground-level, so we were prepared for the weekend work.

Finally, by October, the project was complete just in time for my son's 5th birthday party, and it was massive!

I included some pictures of the treehouse for you at the end of this chapter, trust me, it came in nowhere near budget:>

It has a flight of stairs going up to the 'main' floor of the treehouse, which is about 80 square feet (8' x 10'). Then there is a 6-foot swinging bridge which connects to a second tower that has a walking plank down to yet a third platform where you can access both a slide and climbing wall.

Built in below the swinging bridge of the treehouse is a pair of swings. The entire 'play area' is then surrounded by a rubberized border and filled with safety, fall-rated recycled rubber.

The final project was beautiful, and it transformed our backyard into a park like setting that has received complements during every kid's party and any other events that we have hosted in the 6 years since it has been completed. (Check out the images at the end of this chapter).

The only downside that I did not foresee is the maintenance that is required. We used cedar to build the treehouse, sanded and sealed with outdoor stain. However, being outdoors the stain wears down and needs to be maintained. If it is to last, the treehouse needs to be constantly monitored, and it needs to be occasionally repaired.

It might be odd, but to me it is normal that I think of everything in terms of online advertising.

I was reviewing a Google account a few days ago, and I started thinking how creating an account in Google Merchant Center is much like building a treehouse.

You don't realize how much effort goes into the building it until you start building.

If you do it right, you can be assured it will transform your business. It requires maintenance in order to last.

I'm sure if you are an eCommerce advertiser running Google Shopping, Shopping Actions or Dynamic Remarketing ads you most likely know how much effort it took to create your Google Merchant Center account.

However, how much time do you spend in maintaining your Google Merchant Center account?

One of the main mistakes I come across is advertisers not monitoring and fixing regular errors in your Merchant Center Account.

Just like building my treehouse, this section focuses on what you need to concentrate when setting up and maintaining your Merchant Center account to ensure optimal performance for your Google Ads.

CHAPTER 5

―――――◆―――――

Populating Merchant Center with Proper Data

After your Merchant Center has been approved and you have completed the appropriate settings for shipping, tax, etc. it is a critical time. A time that will play a major part in determining your success using Google Shopping. It is time to create your plan for populating your product data inside Merchant Center.

You will soon discover that having well formatted data is going to be essential in order to properly segment campaigns inside the Google Ads interface.

Updating Product Data in Merchant Center

To get started, you need to submit the products to Merchant Center that you want to have eligible to appear in Google Shopping. When submitting your products, there are four options:

> Google Sheets – You make all of the changes manually to the product data using a Google Sheet. These changes are automatically applied to your account once uploaded.

Schedule fetch – You host a data feed file on your website and schedule a time for Google to fetch updates from the file. Once the fetch occurs, Google applies updates to your products in Merchant Center.

Upload – This is the most common. With this method, you keep the file and schedule a regular upload into your merchant center using SFTP, FTP, Google Cloud storage or a manual upload.

Content API – The Content API for Shopping enables merchants to automatically upload product listings using an API connection.

The Process of Submit Products

Unless you have just a handful of products that rarely change in terms of inventory and pricing it typically is not viable to manually create and update a product feed.

The good news is that there are many 3rd party Data Optimization Companies that specialize in getting data from your website to Merchant Center. The bad news is how do you know which data optimization company is a good fit for your company and for your needs?

The better a data optimization company is the easier they are going to make the process for merchants of taking data in their website and easily customizing that data into Google's different fields.

Here are the different fields that are currently supported in Google Shopping. Not all the fields below are required, but the more fields that you populate, the better Google is going to be able to match your products to relevant customer searches.

link	shipping_label	material
title	product_type	pattern
description	shipping	additional_image_link
price	multipack	age_group
sale_price	is_bundle	gender
sale_price_effective_date	adwords_grouping	adult
mobile_link	adwords_labels	item_group_id
image_link	excluded_destinatino	custom_label_0
id	expiration_datapromotion_id	custom_label_1
brand	availability	custom_label_2
condition	availability_date	custom_label_3
manufacturer	google_product_category	custom_label_4
mpn	color	shipping_height
gtin	size	shipping_width
identifier_exists	size_type	shipping_length
shipping_weight	size_system	

Being able to populate all or at least as many of these fields as possible is why using a 3rd party data optimization company is usually an essential addition to your Google Shopping efforts.

Imagine if you have 5,000 products and after spending hours creating your initial upload you need to make changes to just a couple of these fields. It would take a long time, right?

Changes can be done using a data feed optimization company in a matter for seconds or minutes instead of hours.

Most fields are not required. Only 13 fields are currently required to have products approved in Merchant Center for non-apparel items, and 20 fields are required for apparel items.

Note, some of the required apparel fields are only required in Shopping Actions not to be approved in Google Shopping. For information on Shopping Actions, refer to chapter 19 - *Google's Shopping Actions – Changing The Landscape.*

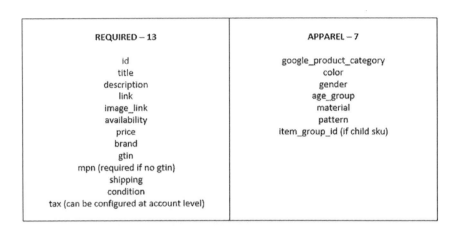

REQUIRED – 13	APPAREL – 7
id	google_product_category
title	color
description	gender
link	age_group
image_link	material
availability	pattern
price	item_group_id (if child sku)
brand	
gtin	
mpn (required if no gtin)	
shipping	
condition	
tax (can be configured at account level)	

Choosing a Data Feed Optimization Company

Now that you have discovered why it is a good idea to partner with a data optimization feed company, how do you select which company is right for your business?

Typically, the price of this service can range from twenty dollars to hundreds of dollars per month, so choosing the right company is going to depend on a few things:

1. Are you planning on using the data feed company to send your product feed to comparison-shopping engines other than Google Shopping? Since Google Shopping is the largest comparison-shopping engine, typically all companies are going to have this feed well structured. The difference with the more expensive companies usually will be in how well they can structure the feeds going to other Shopping portals.

2. How does their system allow you to manipulate your data feed? The main purpose of using a data optimization company is to be able to easily populate your data feed. No matter what company you select, there will be a learning curve; however, make sure you get a full overview as learning how to manipulate and submit your feed is essential.

3. Make sure you know how the company charges. Some data optimization feed companies charge additional fees based on how many products you have. Once you reach a certain number of products, the monthly charge may start increasing.

4. Support is key. There is going to be a learning curve. Make sure whatever data optimization company you select offers full support in helping you get started as well as helping with questions maintaining the health of your data feed moving forward.

5. Make sure you can easily review your feed. As time passes, you are going to want to be able to export your feed. With

some data optimization companies that use an API, I have found that this is not possible.

6. Don't sign a long-term contract! There are so many data optimization companies out there that don't require a long-term commitment. There is no reason to be locked into anything other than a month-to-month agreement.

Working with Your Data

Once you have selected a data optimization company, the first step is importing your products into their system. It is within the data optimization company's system that merchants will format their feed and manipulate the data populating as many of the fields above as possible.

Remember, the more fields you populate, the more effective Google will be in matching your products to related customer inquiries.

Also, start thinking about how it makes sense to segment your products. Google provides the custom label fields in order to help their advertisers segment their data.

The custom label fields serve no purpose in your data feed other than to organize your products, so feel free to enter whatever data you want that will better help you segment your campaigns.

SNEAK PEAK - In the next chapter we will fully explore custom labels including ideas on how to effectively use them.

Submitting Your Feed

Assuming that by now you have already claimed and verified your Merchant Center and have completed your tax and shipping settings, the last piece of completing your merchant center is submit your first product feed.

To begin submitting your first data feed, you will need to navigate under Products in the left-hand menu to 'Feeds' and then click on the blue plus button under Primary feeds.

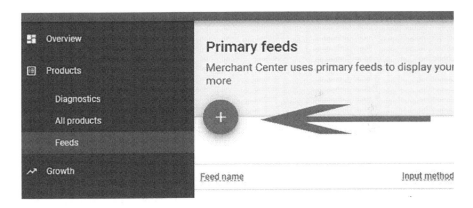

Next, you will select your country of sale, the language for the content of your feed and the destination in Google that you wish your products eligible to appear. As a default, Shopping ads are checked, for information on how to have your products eligible to appear in Shopping Actions, refer later in this book to Chapter 19 - *Google's Shopping Actions – Changing The Landscape.*

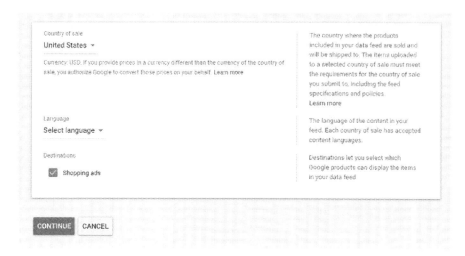

Then, you will name your Primary feed and select the input method. The input method is going to depend upon your data optimization company, but most likely will be the Upload option.

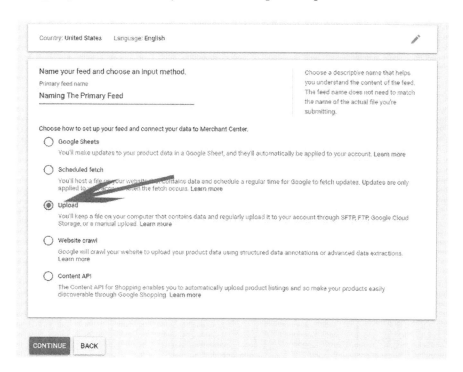

If you select the upload option, you will enter the name and type of file exactly as it will appear coming from your data optimization company. In order to be successfully processed, this must be exact.

In addition, you can upload your new file manually on this page to test if it will be accepted.

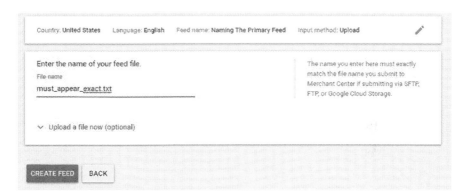

Now that your feed is created there are a couple more items that you will need to format before your feed will be successfully submitted.

First, you will need to provide your data feed optimization company the ability to connect with your Merchant Center account. To do this, you will need to provide them with your Merchant Center SFTP or FTP login credentials. To find these credentials, click on the wrench icon in the top tool bar and choose 'SFTP/FTP/GCS' under 'Settings'.

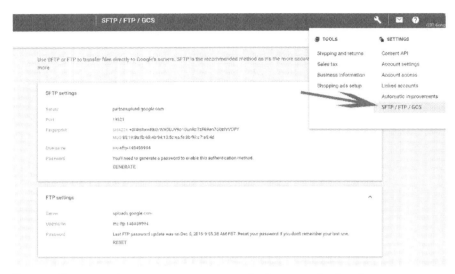

Depending on how your partnered data optimization company connects, this is where you will be able to find the needed credentials.

The last thing that generally causes an initial feed to fail is the merchant not selecting their 'Default currency'. This is the type of currency used to sell products included in the feed.

In order to select, click on your feed name and click on settings. Under 'Default currency' you select your correct currency and save.

That's it. Your feed should now be successful submitted into Google Merchant Center. Google can take up to 72 hours to first process and approve your items, so you will need to be patient. Soon you will be ready for the really fun stuff – setting up your campaigns inside the Google Ads interface!

Final Word

Creating your Merchant Account and formatting your corresponding data feed is going to take some work. However, given that products advertised in Google Shopping are producing some of the highest returns on investment, it is most likely worth the work.

As competition grows for advertisers using Google Shopping, it is going to take more than just sending a partially developed data feed and bidding the same for each item in Google Ads in order to be successful.

However, by fully developing your plan with your data feed, you will gain an immediate advantage over your competitors.

For those of you with a large number of product offerings or product offerings that change frequently, it will be essential to partner with a solid data optimization company. Use the list above in this article to determine the right fit and don't delay. Customers are out there actively searching for your products, and you want to make sure they can find you!

CHAPTER 6

Segmenting Your Product Data – Having A Plan

Pretend that you are a new advertiser and have decided to start advertising using Google Shopping. You have successfully uploaded your products into Google Merchant Center, and you have completed your basic settings. Google has approved all of your products, and you have linked your Merchant Center account to your Google Ads account.

So, you are done, right?

The fact is that although you may be now able to advertise using Google Shopping ads, you are far from done if you wish to run successful Google Shopping campaigns.

Many accounts I have reviewed over the years, unfortunately, stop after the initial setup is complete, leaving a merchant's entire line of products to linger in a single Google Shopping campaign. Running a single Google Shopping Campaign is difficult to optimize and almost impossible to use in order to be able to generate profitable sales.

This article is written for advertisers wishing to squeeze all possible sales and profits out of Google Shopping advertising and discusses why failing to segment their product feed is such a costly mistake.

Why Should You Segment?

When advertising Shopping ads inside of Google Ads, similar to Search ads, advertisers will typically see the best results by segmenting their products into smaller groups of similar products using different Shopping campaigns.

The reason to segment your products is that segmenting allows you to more easily optimize your bidding and control your keywords based on past results. Although these are more advanced concepts, for now, we just need to know that we want to be able to segment our data feed.

For those wanting to skip ahead in the process to discover the cool stuff like how we are going to optimize bidding and control keywords, skip ahead to the advanced section of this book for chapters: Positive Keywords – *A Better Way to Control Unwanted Searches* & *Effectively Optimize Google Shopping Based on Your Past History, Nothing More.*

However, before we can delve into advanced strategies, we need to first set the basics with the best ways to segment your data inside of your Merchant Center feed. Once we have successfully segmented our data, we will have everything we need to fully optimize our advertising inside of the Google Ads interface.

Segmenting – Having A Plan

Let's first quickly review how Google Shopping works:

It Starts With A 'User Query'

Google matches

eligible products in Google Shopping campaigns using

Keywords – Taken from the title and description

then they use a

Real time auction

First and foremost, your products need to be eligible to appear. This means having all of the minimum required data within your data feed including item name, price, image, product id, URL, brand, condition, shipping, tax, gtin or mpn and description.

These are the current basic fields Google requires for non-apparel items. For apparel items, there are even more additional fields including color, gender and age group that are needed.

In addition to all these required fields, Google has another 40 or so fields they use in order to help match products in user queries along with allowing users to filter data in the Google Shopping tab. The more data you submit inside your feed the more likely your products will appear for relevant searches and will increase when they also appear if users are filtering products within Google Shopping.

Populating data into required fields and into suggested fields is a great start; however, our goal as advertisers is not to be able to just advertise it is to be able to advertise and make a profit.

Inside of a product ad group within a Shopping campaign inside the Google Ads interface, advertisers are allowed to subdivide their products by the following fields – Category, Brand, Item ID, Condition, Product Type, Channel, Channel exclusivity or Custom Label 0, Custom Label 1, Custom Label 2, Custom Label 3 or Custom Label 4.

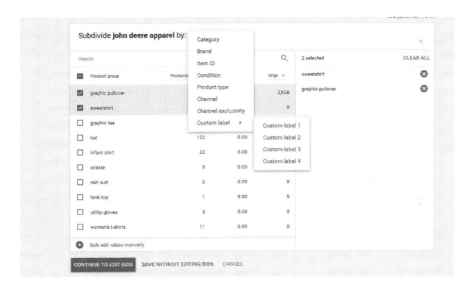

While most data fields are used by Google to match relevant products with users' queries, the only purpose of custom labels is to allow advertisers to add the data, they wish to use in order to be able to subdivide their feed inside of Google Ads.

We will go into step by step detail on how to subdivide product ads in the coming chapter - *How Segmenting Google Shopping Campaigns Can Boost Profitability.*

For now, however, we need to have a plan for deciding what data our custom labels should contain where it will make sense for us to segment.

For my private clients, I typically use custom label 0 and 1 to further identify the item either by name or item type.

For custom label 2, I use as a pricing tier – $0-10; $10-$25; $25-50, etc. This will allow me to implement a tiered bidding strategy.

Finally, for custom labels 3 and 4, I typically use to identify either new items or best-sellers.

Here is a look at mapped custom labels for one of my private clients:

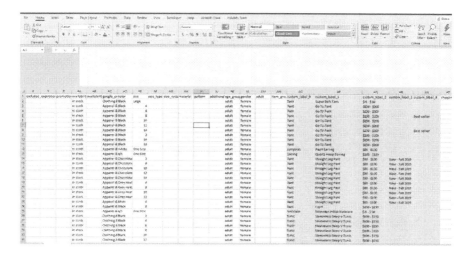

Remember the purpose of adding custom labels are so you can easily segment in order to adjust bids based on sales or spend.

Although your custom labels may vary, this template should serve you as a pretty good roadmap.

Final Word

Being able to control the data in your Google Merchant Center feed is essential to the success of your Google Shopping campaigns. And although implementing advanced strategies such as Positive Keywords, The Adding of Negative Keywords and other optimizations based historical data is much more glamourous and can even be quite fun; first you need to have your data feed properly optimized.

Given this fact, it is important that you get under the hood so to speak and before you start advertising, you first fully understand how Google Shopping ads work.

Second, you must have complete control on your data feed.

Don't worry, there are many great data optimization companies that can help format your data feed and that provide the tools to easily map the feed from data within your website.

However, the strategy of what data to use to populate the custom labels is going to determine how you advertise using Google Shopping, and that is something where the strategy should come from you!

Like any strategy, it shouldn't happen on the fly. Instead, it should be measured and calculated in order to provide the most optimal results. This is why it makes sense to segment your data and then add the custom labels to make segmenting possible.

CHAPTER 7

Enhancing Google Shopping Using Promotions

Google changed their Google Shopping model to a Pay Per Click model in October 2012. Since that change, Google has been extremely focused on providing their users an effective shopping portal that allows consumers to compare prices for the same product among multiple retailers.

Google has added numerous tools that allow advertisers to more effectively market their products and create while helping advertisers differentiate themselves from others selling the same products.

One of the most effective tools for eCommerce advertisers wanting to differentiate from the competition is the ability to add promotions to their products listing on Google Shopping.

Once an advertiser has properly implemented their feed in a Google Merchant Center account and linked the feed to their Google Ads campaigns (see earlier chapters), the advertiser has the ability to add promotions to their products.

Getting Started With Google Promotions

Before advertisers can add a promotion to their products in Google Shopping, they need to request authorization from Google.

In order to be approved, advertisers need to complete the Google Merchant Promotions Interest Form visit-
https://services.google.com/fb/forms/merchantpromotionsform/.
This form requires advertisers to enter their promotions target country, merchant center account number, name, URL homepage and contact information. Once submitted, it usually takes Google approximately 24 hours to review and approve the request. Google will send the contact email confirmation once and if the approval has been granted.

Adding Promotions Once Approved

Once an advertiser has been approved, a new promotions link will appear in the left dashboard of the Google Merchant Center account below the Marketing link. By selecting the Promotions link, advertisers are able to add a variety of promotions to enhance their Google Shopping listings.

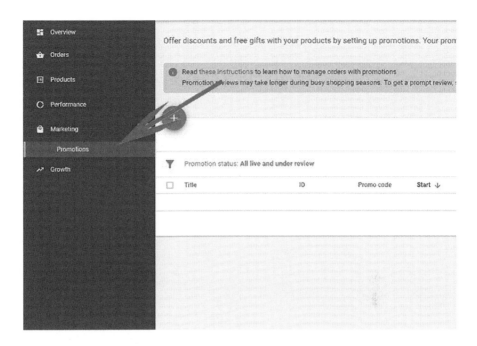

To add a promotion, navigate to the Promotion section and select the blue + button and enter a promotion.

You will be prompted to enter your country/language; destination and promotion category (amount off, percentage off, free gift or free shipping).

Next, you will be prompted to enter a promotion title (describes promotion – shown to customers); a promotion id (used for internal tracking – NOT shown to customers), designate which products are eligible for the promotion, enter the promo code (if needed) and your start and end dates.

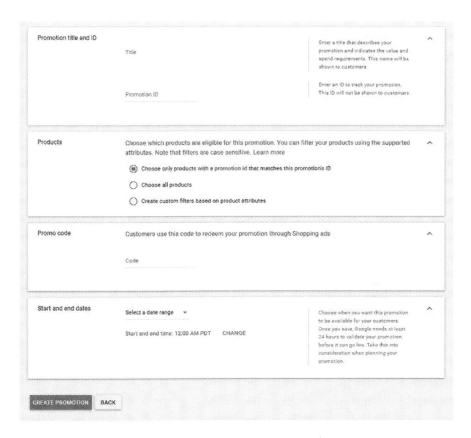

Once you click on the CREATE PROMOTION button, you are set.

Google will review the promotion, which includes both a policy review as well as a validation review.

If the promotion complies with Google guidelines, the promotion should be approved and will become active for product ads in either Google Shopping, Shopping Actions or both (depending on which was selected while creating the promotion). In general, the approval process takes less than 24 hours, and the advertiser will receive an email notification once approval has or has not been granted.

Google Restrictions For Promotions

The following are the current Google requirements for having a promotion approved.

1. The title of the promotion must contain the value of the promotion, and the text may not exceed 60 characters.

2. The title cannot be misleading. It must specifically and clearly state the promotion. Example of a valid promotion: Save 10% On Entire Order. Example of an invalid promotion, Save Up To 10%.

3. If there is a maximum discount threshold, it must be clearly stated. Example, Save 10% On Entire Order (max discount $30).

4. Title cannot include expiration dates. Example, Save 10% On Entire Order – Ends 3/31/15. Don't worry, there is a field to enter when the promotion begins and ends when creating the promotion.

5. Promotion title must be concise and cannot contain extra text. Example of what is not allowed includes a promotion such as: See Why We Can't Be Beat – Save 10%.

6. Promotions must have proper formatting. Proper grammar, spelling and punctuation are required in order for a promotion to be approved.

7. Finally, the promotion must use a coupon that is not currently found on your website. For example, if a merchant offers free shipping on orders over $49 automatically in their

shopping cart, they cannot simply run a promotion for it. The promotion must be unique and require a coupon code.

Example of a Live Promotion

Below is an example of an eCommerce retailer, Epic Sports, using a Google Shopping promotion. Notice the tag with the Special offer next to it? That is a Google shopping promotion live.

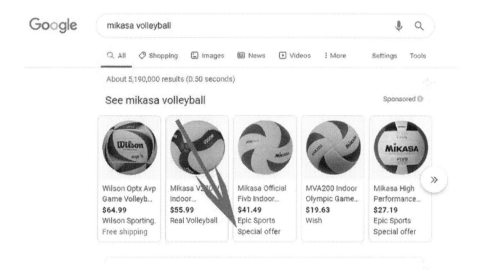

If a user clicks on the 'Special offer' link a window is displayed showing the full promotion.

The promotion displays the name of the company, the offer, when it expires and how to redeem. In this case, the promotion expires in 13 days and to redeem, a user would enter the coupon code listed during checkout.

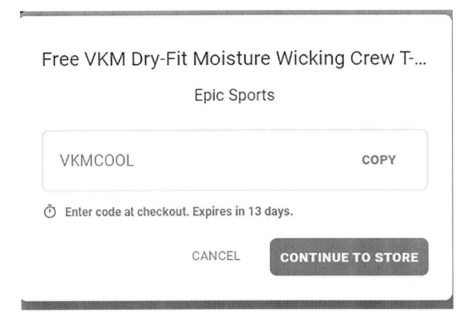

Note, a retailer is not charged when the promotion is displayed. Only if the item URL is clicked or the CONTINUE TO STORE button is clicked after the promotion is opened, then will an advertiser incur their normal charge for the click.

In this example, the retailer is offering a free gift with purchase of a free VKM Dry-Fit Moisture Wicking T-shirt. Offering a free gift with purchase is just one of the options when offering a promotion.

It also doesn't mean that a customer automatically gets the free gift, but they would have to add it to their cart and then apply the promotional code provided. By just having the promotion, this retailer's ad is highlighting their product and thus most likely improving their CTR (click through rates).

Final Word

Typically, Google Shopping typically provides a better ROI and CPA compared to traditional search ads. However, as more and more merchants come to discover this fact, it is essential for advertisers to find ways to have their products stand out from their competitors. A Google promotion allows just that. By adding a promotion that is cost effective, an advertiser can capture more clicks, leading to a higher quality score resulting in a lower average cost per click and the ability to drive more profitable traffic.

A well-run promotion helps to boost click-through rates (CTR); highlight Shopping ads and increase conversions by giving customers a reason to buy now.

Will a promotion work for your company? It depends on the promotion and on the company, but it is a tool definitely worth testing as we all strive to fully optimizing our Google Ads campaigns.

SECTION 3

Optimizations Inside
the Google Ads Interface

What do you think is worse? Taking a strong punch to the gut or receiving a thousand paper cuts? Truth is that both are probably very painful in their own way. Also painful is a poorly optimized Google Shopping Campaign.

Let me explain…

When it comes to a poorly optimized Google Shopping Campaign, typically it is more of the thousand paper cuts scenario. While there is not a single switch to turn on or off that which will stop the financial bleeding, there is an array of factors that generally causes the slow bleeding to your bank account. Those small cuts will eat into your potential profits when using Google Shopping every day, 24 hours a day, seven days a week!

There are literally thousands of paper cuts that can cost a Google Ads account to bleed money. This chapter addresses the major bleeds that I come across way too often when performing personal Google Ads Assessments for customers. This includes:

1. Not segmenting Google campaigns. Instead of segmenting, many marketers new to Google Shopping simply will group all their products into one campaign and never touch them again. This section details how to segment and optimize your campaigns and why it is important to do so.

2. Not adjusting mobile bids. This is an easy fix if analytics is properly installed. It also is a relatively quick fix. Mobile clicks seldom have the same conversion rates or the same average conversion value as desktop bids, and bidding the same across all devices is one of those papercuts that really hurts!

3. Set It & Forget It – Just because you optimized your campaign fully last week, last month or even last year, in no way does that mean that your account is still running at an optimal level today. The bullseye is always changing when it comes to finding the right bids on the right devices and using the right keywords when it comes to using Google and Google Shopping.

Unfortunately, many business owners are unable (due to time or due to lack of knowledge) to spend the time it takes to keep their accounts running at an optimal level. I can't remember first reviewing a Google Ads account that doesn't have room for improvement and typically, lots of improvement. With so many moving parts, Google Ads and, in particular, Google Shopping can be difficult to manage unless you or someone on your team has spent years going through the 'Google Learning Curve'.

This chapter is focused on the major optimizations that can be done inside your account in order to start pulling maximum profits from your Shopping campaigns.

CHAPTER 8

How Segmenting Google Shopping Campaigns Can Boost Profitability

Google Shopping has the potential to produce one of the highest returns on investment (ROI) for ecommerce retailers advertising online. For those new to online marketing, that is a good thing, in fact, perhaps the most important thing!!! A high ROI means that the money that is invested in a marketing channel is generating a high return of sales for the investment.

ROI Calculation =

(Gain from investment – Cost of Investment) / Cost of Investment

Over the last few years, I have consistently seen clients' Google Shopping campaigns attain a higher ROI than that attained from either Google Search or Display (retargeting) advertising, making it an important part of Google advertising for ecommerce retailers. However, being able to achieve a really high ROI can typically only be attained through properly segmenting your Google Shopping campaigns.

A Quick Review - How Google Shopping Works

Google Shopping results are displayed at the very top of the page before the organic listings (as seen in the example below). Google Shopping results can also be viewed inside Google when a shopper clicks on the Shopping tab in the upper menu next to the default 'All' link.

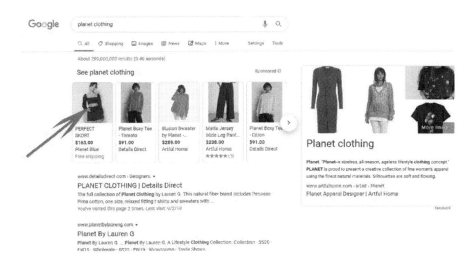

When deciding which products to display, Google uses a real-time auction system just like search results to list products in Google Shopping. In order for products to appear, the products must be included within a merchant's approved Google Merchant Center Account. The Merchant Center account must also be actively linked to an active Shopping campaign within the Google Ads interface.

Once connected to a Google Merchant Center account containing approved products, Google allows advertisers to subdivide their product listings based on populated fields contained within their submitted products in their Merchant Center account.

In addition, Google also allows advertisers to add promotions to their Google Shopping listings, which is another great way to increase click through rates (CTR). Note, Google promotions are added through the Merchant Center account as well and not within the Google Ads interface. The last chapter discussed details and best-practices on creating promotions. If you skipped ahead and are interested in promotions, please go back and read.

However, even if you have a Google Shopping campaign that is being optimized and you are running meaningful promotions, there remains a problem. If all Shopping listings are contained within the same campaign, advertisers are restricted because they must have the same settings across the entire campaign.

What this means for advertisers is that they can, of course, adjust bids inside the campaign as a whole based on location, ad schedule, devices, but what if they want to change settings, thus affecting bids on different products or a category of products? Of course, they cannot if all of their products are contained within a single campaign.

This is why segmenting Shopping campaigns is essential for many retailers if they wish to fully optimize their Google Shopping listings based on location, time of day or devices. One of the most important concepts to grasp for those just starting to use Google Shopping, segmenting Shopping campaigns is probably the most important factor advertisers can do when wanting to improving Shopping results and if done right will provide advertisers a distinct advantage over their competitors.

Creating Multiple Google Shopping Campaigns

The first step in creating a new Shopping campaign containing a sub-section of a feed's product offerings is to create a new Shopping campaign. In order to do so while in the Campaigns view, click on the blue plus button and select New Campaign.

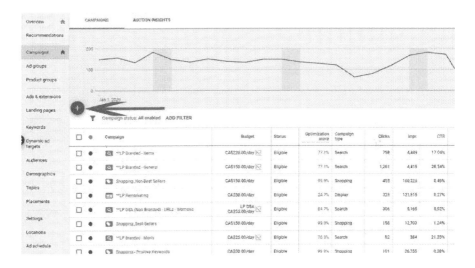

Next, you will select the campaign's goal. For Shopping campaigns, you will select 'Sales' and the blue 'Continue' button.

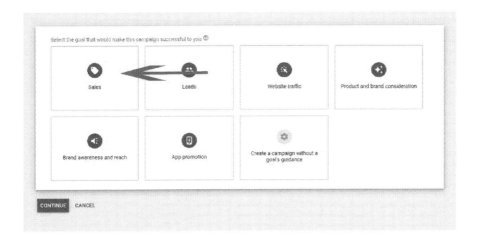

Then, you will need to select the new campaign type. For Shopping campaigns, you will want to select Shopping and the blue 'Continue' button.

You will then need to select which Merchant Center account you wish to link your campaign; select the country where products are being sold and whether you want to run a Google Smart Shopping campaign or a Standard Shopping campaign. (Note, this selection cannot be changed once a campaign is created).

For my private clients, I manage Standard Shopping campaigns, as it gives you more control over where and at what costs your Shopping ads will appear. However, be careful because Google defaults your option to the newly released Smart Shopping campaign.

For information on Smart Shopping campaigns and why I recommend that most advertisers stay away, see chapter 17 - *New Google Smart Shopping Campaigns – What You Need to Realize.*

Google will then prompt you to name your new campaign, set your budget, select your bidding strategy and decide if you would like to use Google's Enhanced CPC to automatically raise your maximum bid if a click seems likely to lead to a conversion.

Next is a setting named Campaign priority. You will find this setting useful when segmenting your products within campaigns.

The default on Campaign priority is Low. Best-practices would recommend that this setting be changed to either Medium or High since it contains a sub-set of the full product offering.

This setting is a safeguard. If a product is contained within multiple campaigns, the product will be shown depending on which campaign has the higher bid. However, if a product is in multiple campaigns where there are different priority levels, the priority level is the determining factor for which campaign the product will be pulled.

Finally, you will want to specify in which Networks you want your products to be eligible to be displayed. This is a fairly new option. Until recently, Google Shopping ads would only display within the Search Network. Now, the default is to have Shopping ads appear within the YouTube and Discover Network as well. This is a great option for increased exposure, but I have found that these placements do not generate near the ROI of having products appear only within the Search Network.

Finally, select which location to serve your ads, the start and end dates of your campaign and click on the blue 'Save and Continue' button.

You will then be asked to select some settings for your first Ad Group including the Ad Group Type, Ad Group Name and your initial bid.

Note, the Ad Group Type – Product Shopping is the standard Shopping Ad and what I recommend for private clients.

Finally, we are ready to start determining which products should be in the campaign. By default, when an advertiser creates a new campaign, Google brings in the entire product offering in the data feed linked from the advertiser's merchant center account.

However, the point of segmenting is to include a subset of products within the new campaign. In order to subdivide, click on the + symbol next to the All products.

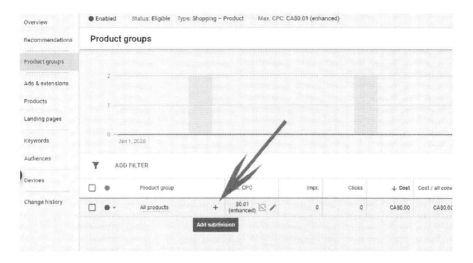

A window will then pop-up allowing retailers to subdivide according to fields they have populated within their products that are currently approved within Google Merchant Center Account.

In the example below, I am looking at the feed subdivided by Custom_label 0, which for this particular feed contains the different categories as seen on the website.

In order to add a subsection, simply click the box adding a checkmark to the right of the name and click 'Continue To Edit Bids'. Note, multiple categories can be selected if an advertiser wishes to use the same settings for all subsections that are to be included within the new campaign.

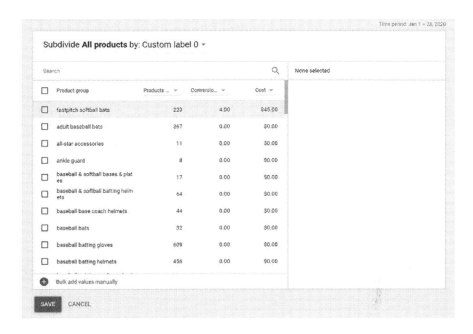

Once a subsection has been added, advertisers can adjust their bid on the entire product group.

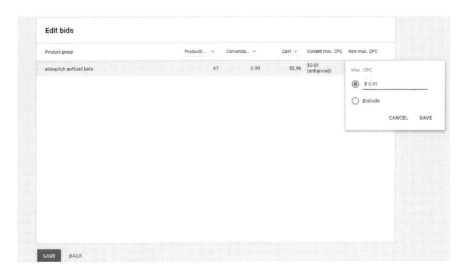

Once the subsection is added and saved, a campaign will show the subsection(s) along with another subsection named Everything else. Since we are subdividing, and the rest of the products are found within the main Shopping campaign, we will not want the rest of the products or 'Everything else' displaying within this campaign. Therefore, we need to exclude those products.

To exclude, simply click on the bid column next to the product group that should be excluded and select the radio button next to Excluded and save.

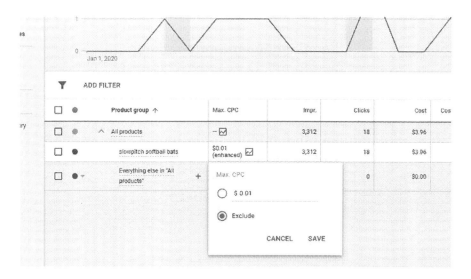

Once you have saved properly, there should be the word Excluded grayed out next to the Product Group that is no longer eligible to display within this campaign.

That is it, the new campaign has been created with the desired subsection of products, and settings can now be optimized based on these products rather than by all products that were originally in the main Shopping campaign.

A best-practices tip here - although setting a high priority level setting should prevent products being shown in other campaigns, I always recommend excluding the newly created subsection in other lower priority campaigns where you do not wish for product ads to be shown. In order to exclude those products, navigate to the main Shopping campaign and follow the same steps as above, only this time excluding the subsection that is now in the new Shopping campaign.

Final Word

Obviously, the newly created campaign will not have historical data needed to optimize, but it will populate over time. Once the data starts coming in, there are three important ways to change bids based on results all which have the potential for impactful results in the new campaign. These three ways to optimize include: Locations, Ad Schedule and Devices.

If you have taken time to have a plan when mapping out your data, you will most likely find that the way you want to optimize these areas of bidding along with the negative keywords that you add will be different between campaigns. Being different is one of the reasons why it makes sense to segment product data into different campaigns. For those with a substantial number of product offerings, just like classic search campaigns, segmenting your product offerings will greatly outperform a non-segmented campaign.

With Shopping ads, Display ads (particularly retargeting) along with Search ads, advertisers have the ability to advertise their product offerings in a variety of different ways.

When deciding which method of advertising is viable for an advertiser's business goals, an advertiser must closely monitor results in terms of costs vs sales in order to optimize accounts that generate the most profitable ROI.

Google Shopping is an effective tool for doing this, but it must be properly configured in order to fully optimize results. Segmenting

Shopping campaigns with the steps above is an advanced technique that can help to generate an ROI, but like the setup of most campaigns, requires work and constant monitoring. Perhaps this is why it has the ability to generate such great results, because the vast number of advertisers are not making the effort to employ this tactic. Thus, leaving opportunity for those who are willing to put in the effort to fully market their products using all the tools available in Google's every changing Ads platform.

CHAPTER 9

Adjusting Google Shopping Bids
for Individual Products

Even though an individual campaign may be showing overall profitable results, if you dig into a campaign, you most likely will find products that are converting well below your average cost per acquisition and some that are converting well above (the 80/20 rule).

* The 80/20 rule with Google Shopping is that typically 20% of all your products make up 80% of both your costs and your sales.

However, and this is assuming you have already segmented your Google Shopping campaigns. Given that you have based on the last chapter, how do you optimize individual product bids for Google Shopping ads inside those segmented campaigns?

First, your campaigns must have enough historical data to be relevant in your decisions. Google provides several competitive metrics advertisers can use when deciding whether to raise or lower bids for individual products appearing within Google Shopping. These competitive metrics include Benchmark CTR, Benchmark Max CTR, Search Imp Share, Search Lost IS (rank) and Click share.

In order to enable various competitive metrics to display while in the Campaigns view, click on the 'Columns' button and select 'Modify columns'.

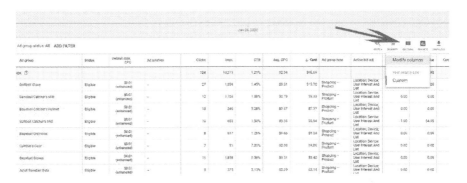

Once the modify columns window opens, an advertiser needs to select 'Competitive metrics' under the 'Select metrics' columns and add each competitive metric that they wish to view.

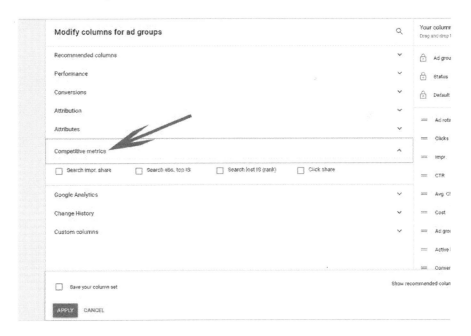

Here are the more important metrics to view when deciding whether to raise or lower an individual product bid:

Search Imp Share – The impressions your products have received divided by the estimate number of impressions your products were eligible to receive (available for both the product group and the individual item level).

Search abs. top IS – Short for 'Search absolute top impression share,' this is the percentage of your Search ad impressions that are shown in the most prominent Search position.

Search Lost IS (rank) – Short for 'Search lost impressions share,' this is the percentage of impressions your ads did not receive due to poor Ad Rank or insufficient bidding (available for both the product group and the individual item level).

Click Share – The clicks you received on Google's Search Network divided by the maximum number of clicks that you could have received (available for both the product group and the individual item level).

For optimizing an individual product bid, I prefer to look at the Search Impr. Share in conjunction with Cost, Avg. CPC and Conversions.

Below are some examples of how I use these metrics to determine when to raise, lower or keep current Shopping bids for individual products:

When to Raise a Product Bid

When there is sufficient historical data, Google will add a small graph next to an individual product's Max. CPC column that when accessed will display how many impressions and clicks an advertiser can expect to receive by adjusting their bid for any product.

When optimizing products in Google Shopping manually, I tend to look for products with conversions that have a relatively low Avg. CPC where the Search Impr. share is below 50%.

Below, the product 'a1010blem' has a bid of $0.59, with six conversions in the last 2 weeks and a Search Impr. share of under 50%. In addition, the six conversions have generated a total of $2,112.25 in total sales on a spend of $23.26 for a ROAS of a whopping 89.18.

This historical data makes this product an excellent candidate to investigate whether raising the product bid is viable.

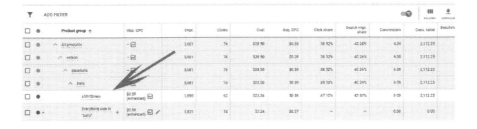

By clicking on the small graph icon, Google opens a Bid Simulator window that shows what clicks, costs and impressions this item can expect if the bid is changed to one of the bid options listed. This is where experience comes into play. I typically will raise the bid to a level that makes sense based on past experience managing similar products within the account.

Here, by raising the bid from $0.59 to $1.10, we will see our search impression share increase to 78.10% and our click share increase to 81.52%.

Quick note, raising bids is a great way to bring more traffic to a product that has historically done well in terms of conversions, but it will also increase your spend and may result in products being displayed for a broader range of search terms. It is highly recommended to continually monitor changes (especially when raising bids) to maintain levels of profitability.

When to Lower a Product Bid

Conversely, sometimes it is necessary to lower a specific product bid that is receiving clicks, but zero or few conversions.

Below is an item 'ckcc1216s7x-black', where the bid is at $1.25, the search impression share is 89.38% and the average CPC is $0.60. This product has received 131 clicks and incurred a cost of $79.21 over the last two weeks.

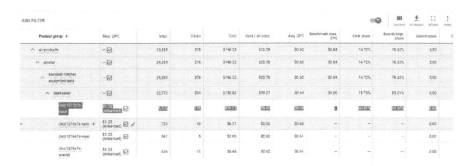

After checking to ensure there are no issues on the website or in the Merchant Center account, thus ensuring that there is no issue with the product, I decide to lower the bid.

By again clicking on the small graph icon located next to the Max. CPC field, I can view Google recommendations of how many clicks, impressions and costs I can expect the item to incur by lowering the bid.

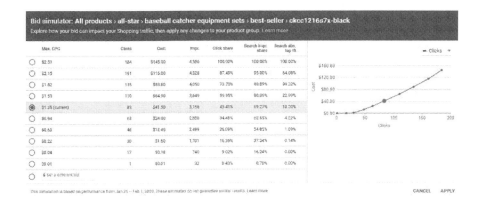

In this instance, I am going to lower the bid from $1.25 to $0.94. This will still allow this product to still receive some clicks and impressions; however, the product will be shown less often, allowing other products in this subsegment to appear more often for the same keyword searches. I will continue to monitor and review the bid once additional historical data is available based on the newly adjusted bid.

When Not to Adjust a Product Bid

For advertisers, just as important as raising and lowering individual bids is determining when NOT to adjust a bid for a particular product.

Below, the product 'cpcc1216s7x-maroon' has a bid of $1.25, with 2 conversion in the last 2 weeks; $47.33 in spend and revenue generated of $239.90. This calculates to a ROAS of 5.07.

With all the criteria I use to raise a bid, I would like to view how many additional impressions, clicks and costs Google expects this product to receive if I raise the bid. Therefore, again I click on the graph icon next to the Max. CPC field.

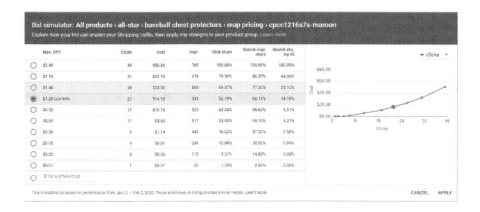

For this item, even if I increase the bid approximately 50% from the current $1.25 to $1.74, it would only add about 150 more impressions but would double spend from $16.10 to $32.10 (almost 100%).

Also, keep in mind that this is raising the Max CPC. When looking at historical data, I can realize that this product has been actually incurring an average CPC of $0.83 per click. With this information available, I decide that raising the bid is not a good value and that it does NOT make sense to raise the bid and will leave the bid at $1.25.

Profitability Report

The process of manually adjusting bids works great if you need to optimize a handful of products, but what if you have hundreds or even thousands of products that you want to optimize for profitability?

For accounts with large offerings, I use a self-created process that I have aptly named my 'Profitability Report'.

Automated rules are not available for Google Shopping items. Therefore, the purpose of the profitability report is to naturally raise product bids for items that convert, while lowering bids for items that are not converting using a systematic formula.

Creating the Profitability Report

1. Click on reports icon in top tool bar.

2. Select Predefined Reports > Shopping > Shopping – Item ID.

3. This should populate the following key performance indicators (KPIs): Item ID, Clicks, Impressions, CTR, Avg CPC, Costs, Cost/Conv and Conv. Rate.

4. You will then want to add Conversion Value, Campaign and Ad Group. Note, adding a column is done by dragging the desired field from the left menu to the table. It may be necessary to click on the three horizontal lines to display all options.

5. Save As 'Profitability Report.'

6. Note, once the repot is saved, you can schedule the created report to automatically run so next time the report will be available in advance.

Using the Profitability Report

1. Click on reports icon in top tool bar.

2. Download the profitability report for the desired date range (suggestion is weekly or bi-weekly).

3. Create a new column for rate on ad spend (ROAS) – conversion value/costs.

4. This is where some discretion comes as far as optimizing and campaign goals including the overall profitability you are trying to achieve. For the accounts that I privately manage, if the ROAS is between 2 -5, I raise by 20%; if between 5-10, I raise 35%; if over 10, I raise 50%. For most of my accounts, I use a $5 threshold for costs; however, this can be adjusted depending on the accounts volume.

5. To make it easier, I add a comment field with the action to click on the item and highlight with a color – example: green for all items that need to be raised.

ROAS Formula

ROAS =
Conv Value/Costs

Action

ROAS 2-5 > 20%

ROAS 5-10 > 35%

ROAS over 10 >
50%

Costs over $10 with
0 conversions < 25%

Costs over $5 with 0
– conversions < 15%

6. Next, I sort by poor performing item ids. To do this, sort by cost from largest to smallest.

7. Set your criteria. For example, in the accounts I manage, I lower bids by 25% on any item that spends over $10 with $0 sales and lower bids by 10% on any item that spends over $5 with $0 sales. Again, I color code the items that need to be decreased in order to easily determine.

8. I then sort the excel sheet by Notes and then Ad Group.

9. You now have an easy to read file where you can make actionable changes.

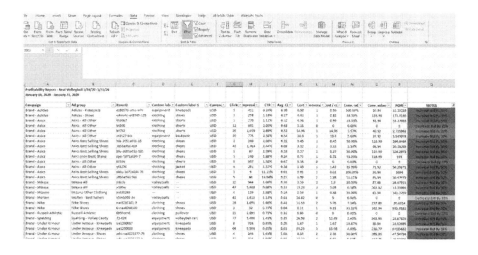

Final Word

Optimizing bids for individual products can be a labor-intensive process. However, it also can be a rewarding process in gaining the highest return on advertising spend (ROAS) available for your dollars. In addition, there are other factors to consider before raising or lowering a product bid such as: is the product in stock, is the product a seasonal seller and are there other factors that can account for increase/decrease sales such as a competitor discounting?

However, by taking advantage of Google's competitive metrics, advertisers can optimize their Shopping Campaigns at the product level. Quick warning, for this strategy to be the most effective, advertisers should ensure they have previously segmented their Shopping Campaigns as we discussed in the last chapter.

CHAPTER 10

The Art of Adding Negative Keywords

One of the quickest and most effective ways for advertisers to optimize their Google Ads account is with the proper use of negative keywords. A powerful optimizing tool for both Shopping and Search campaigns, negative keywords work to block unwanted search terms from triggering ads to be shown.

Let's quickly review what Google keywords are before looking at negative keywords.

For Google shopping campaigns, there are no keywords. Google matches keywords found in an advertiser's product titles and descriptions and matches them to related user queries. The lack of keywords makes using negative keywords, especially in shopping campaigns, a must for advertisers to prevent product ads from appearing for irrelevant searches.

Google search campaigns are more straightforward. Keywords are created within the Google ads account added by the advertiser, and these keywords fully dictate which search terms trigger ads to appear. Negative keywords are still important, especially if advertisers are using match types other than Exact Match.

Currently, Google supports five different types of keywords for Search campaigns: Exact Match, Phrase Match, Broad Match, Broad Match Modifier and Negative keywords.

Regardless of campaign type, negative keywords have the top hierarchy of the different types of keywords. Adding a negative keyword to an advertiser's account, campaign or ad group will block all ads from being displayed even if that same keyword is also listed as one of the other keyword types for a search campaign.

However, although the negative keyword will block ads from being shown, having a keyword as both a negative and either an exact, phrase, broad or broad match modifier keyword in a search campaign will trigger a Google alert and is not recommended.

How Do You Know Which Negative Keywords to Add?

In order to determine if it is necessary to add negative keywords, review your search terms report in order to discover which keywords are driving traffic.

Effectively using Search Terms is an entirely different subject on which I have dedicated the next entire chapter - *Keyword Search Terms – Unlocking The Google Ads Puzzle.*

For now, we are going to assume you have a list of negative keywords you would like to add. Common negative keywords across accounts include keywords such as: free, coupon, pictures, cheap, wholesale, etc. Therefore, we will use these keywords in our example.

Adding Negative Keywords at the Ad Group & Campaign Levels

Once you have your list of negative keywords, they can be added for the ad group, campaign or account level. We will look at how to properly add negative keywords at all 3 levels and strategies to implement.

The process for adding negative keywords to either the ad group or campaign levels is identical and will depend on whether you are viewing the campaign or ad group level.

In order to add negative keywords at either the ad group or campaign level, first navigate to either the ad group or campaign you wish to add the negative keyword(s) and click on the Negative Keywords link in the left-hand column below the Keywords link. (You may need to click on the small arrow to the left of the Keywords link in order to view the Negative Keywords).

The negative keywords view will show all existing negative keywords currently applied to this campaign including which negative keyword, where they are added, the level (account, campaign or ad group) and the match type for the negative keyword.

In order to add additional negative keywords at either the campaign or ad group, an advertiser will first click on the blue plus button.

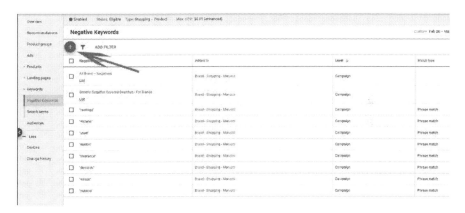

This will open a new window where advertisers can add their desired negative keywords.

Here advertisers are allowed to either manually enter new negative keywords or apply a negative keyword list (we will discuss this later in this article). In addition, advertisers can decide whether to add the negative keywords to either the campaign or ad group level.

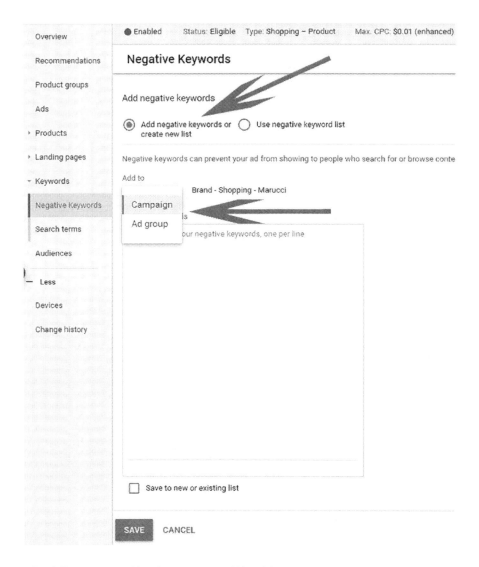

If adding manually, here you will add the negative keywords. By including either within brackets, quotes or with no punctuation will determine the negative keyword match type.

Exact Negative - Brackets – Excludes all searches from appearing that contain that exact search.

Phrase Negative – Quotes – Excludes all searches from appearing that contain the negative phrase.

Broad Negative – Nothing – Excludes all searches from appearing that contains that word or words.

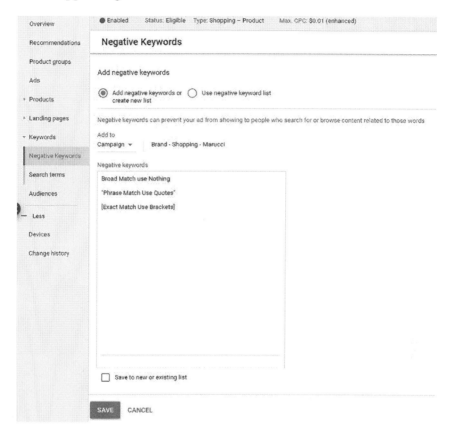

Adding Negative Keywords at the Account Level

Adding a list of negative keywords at the account level will limit ads being triggered throughout the account.

A distinct advantage of adding negative keywords at the account level is a quick and semi-easy way to limit unwanted traffic for generic terms that advertisers wish never to be able to trigger their ads across their account.

In order to add negative keywords at the account level, the first step is to click on the Negative Keyword lists located under the Shared library section under Tools and Settings.

Then, click on blue plus button to add a new negative keyword list or click on an existing list to modify the keywords currently contained within a list.

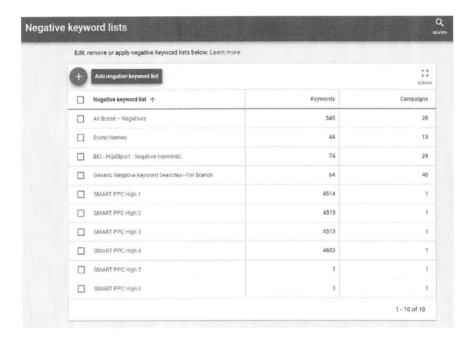

To add a new negative keyword list, click on the blue plus button; add your negative keywords; name the list and then save.

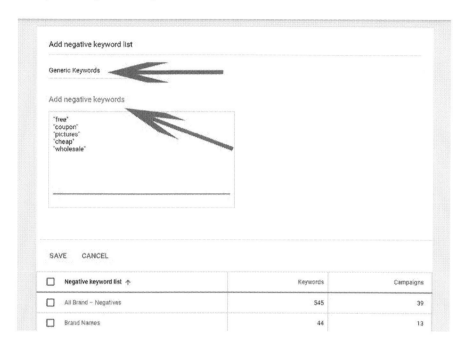

Once you create or when you are using an existing negative keyword list, advertisers can easily apply the list to multiple campaigns.

To apply to multiple campaigns, first click on the negative keyword list you would like to apply. Then, you will be either allowed to add more negative keywords or to apply the list to one or more existing campaigns. In order to add to campaigns, click on the blue 'Apply to Campaigns'.

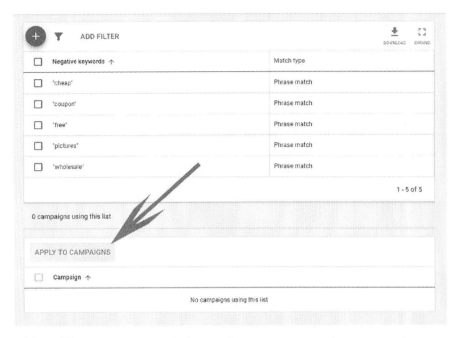

This will open a new window where you can select campaigns to apply your negative keyword list. Simply select the box next to the campaign or campaigns that you wish to add the list and click the 'Done' button.

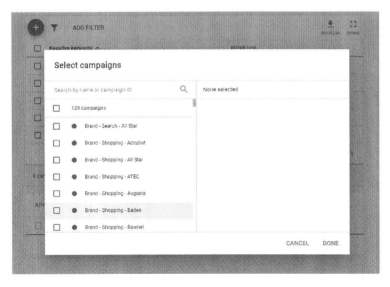

Remember that you can also apply a negative keyword list directly within the campaign where you add individual negative keywords (see instructions above).

Final Word

The proper use of negative keywords is a powerful tool in optimizing an advertiser's campaign. By examining past account performance, an advertiser can find a list of keywords that, if properly implemented, will stop ads from being displayed for non-relevant search terms.

Properly optimized, keeping up to date with negative keywords is a best-practice that not only can substantially save ad budget, but will also make your ads more relevant, thus helping improve overall metrics in an account.

Keep in mind with negative keywords that once you are done, you are not done. The use of negative keywords is NOT a set it and forget it technique.

In order to get the most out of an ads budget, a properly optimized account will need an advertiser continuing to search, discover and implement new negative keywords on an ongoing basis throughout the lifetime of the account.

CHAPTER 11

Keyword Search Terms
– Unlocking the Ads Puzzle

Regardless of which type of advertising medium you use to run your ads, one truth is essential to your success: you must be able to track response including when, where and how potential customers responded to your ad.

For off-line advertising, this may be a bit broader, such as which magazine or newspaper on which date did a customer respond to your ad. This is traditionally tracked by using a special trackable URL or trackable phone number specific for each location the ad appears.

Fortunately, for us who advertise using PPC, tracking can be pinpointed down to the exact search terms a customer used to find your ad along with a slew of other data, including the exact time your ad was clicked and the device the potential customer used to click on your ad.

To access this information in Google, one must become familiar with the Search Terms report.

Growing up, I loved working with puzzles with the challenge of having all the pieces fit together to create something that sometimes could be pretty amazing, if I say so myself.

Google Ads is a puzzle. The Search Terms report, for advertisers who discover which search terms are leading to their ads being shown, is a big piece of unlocking the Google Ads puzzle regardless of whether your campaign is a Search or a Shopping campaign.

This is where you are spending the money, so you need to know on what. Think of advertising on Google as a purchase of sorts, which, in fact, it is as you are purchasing traffic.

You wouldn't go to the grocery store with a list and come out with a random bag of groceries, would you?

Of course not, you need specific items.

Well, you are purchasing traffic, and you want to make sure you are getting specific traffic and nothing else is sneaking into your bag (back to the grocery metaphor).

By reviewing your search terms campaign regularly, an advertiser can reveal instant information about the quality of their PPC traffic.

This information can be most useful to discover the following:

1. What search terms are converting.

2. Which search terms are receiving traffic but are not converting.

3. Whether or not search terms advertisers feel are relevant are generating traffic.

We will review why each of the reasons is important along with what to do with what you discover, but first we need to see where to access the user search terms report that shows which terms are generating traffic to your ads.

Here are the steps:

1. Open any campaign or ad group (note, keywords can be viewed at the account, campaign or ad group level).

2. Click on the 'Keywords' link in the left menu.

3. Click on the 'Search Terms' link below. (For Shopping campaigns, the sub-menu under Keywords only has Negative Keywords and Search Terms. For Search campaigns, the sub-menu under Keywords contains Search Keywords, Negative Keywords, Search Terms and Auction Insights).

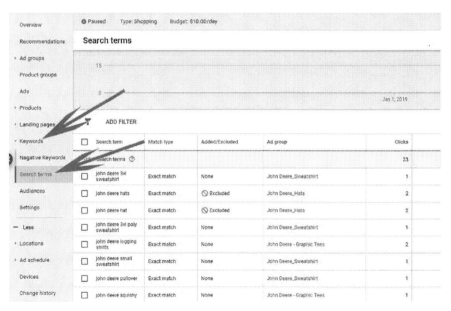

Search Terms That Are Converting – Shopping Campaigns

The way to handle search terms that are converting is going to be different depending on whether you are optimizing a Shopping campaign or a Search campaign. It is also going to depend on if you are looking at the Search Terms report at the Account, Campaign or Ad Group level.

In order to be the most beneficial, especially when there are a substantial number of conversions, you are going to want to look at the most granular data possible, which means looking at the Search Terms report at the Ad Group level.

One of the most effective ways to use the Search Terms report is in discovering which keyword searches are converting and for which of your products. You can also view your click-through-rate (CTR) of any keyword searches. CTR is calculated by dividing Clicks by Impressions.

If you discover a search term that has conversions; however, it has a relatively low CTR, this is a great indicator that you may want to consider changing either your product title or product description.

Since only the product title, image, price and retailer name is shown in a Google Shopping ad, modifying your product title to closely relate to the search terms that have historically converted will help to improve your CTR as well to help increase your conversion rate for those keyword searches.

Search Terms That Are Not Converting – Shopping Campaigns

With Shopping campaigns, when your products appear in searches is based on Google's algorithm that matches your item title and description along with your bid to a customer's search.

Many times, this can lead to your product ads appearing for irrelevant terms.

By using the Search Terms report, an advertiser can easily identify those terms that are spending ad budget but not converting into sales.

Once non-converting search terms are identified, advertisers can add these search terms as negative keywords at the ad group, campaign or even account level. In addition, non-converting search terms can be added to a negative keyword list, making it easier to apply across multiple campaigns.

Just like search terms, negative keywords can be added in an exact, phrase or broad match type.

For details on adding negative keywords, again, review the last chapter - *The Art of Adding Negative Keywords*.

Are Relevant Keyword Searches Generating Traffic? – Shopping Campaigns

Assuming you have done your homework and researched keywords, the Search Terms report is a great place to determine whether researched keywords are generating traffic and whether they are generating sales.

If you have identified through keyword research a keyword that historically has quite a bit of traffic on Google but is not generating traffic to your campaign, there are typically two main culprits.

First, Google does not deem your product to be relevant to that search term. In order to remedy this issue, you will need to either change your product title, description or both to be more relevant for the keyword that you are trying to gain traffic. By making your product listings more relevant for a targeted keyword, you increase the chances of your product ads appearing for a specific search term.

Second, your bid is too low and therefore not competitive. If your product is optimized for a keyword and is still not appearing or at least not appearing often, your bid may be too low. In order to see if this is the case, you can either use Google's bid adjuster to see what Google recommends for a bid or you can view your search impression share for a particular product ad that you believe should be receiving more traffic.

Final Word

Think of running a successful Google Shopping Campaign as a big puzzle. Trying to determine what you are spending money on, where you should increase what you are spending and where you should decrease what you are spending is a huge part of completing your puzzle.

By effectively using the Keywords Search Terms report, advertisers have a tool to complete this puzzle. However, the keywords search terms report needs to be monitored, because keywords that convert can change and non-relevant keyword searches that cause product ads to appear are an on-going issue within both your campaigns and ad groups.

The good news is that by monitoring your Keywords Search Terms report with an effective plan of action, you can optimize for more profitability and effectively work to stay ahead of your competitors using Google Ads.

CHAPTER 12

Effectively Optimize Google Shopping Based on Past History Nothing More

Most retailers are not profitable advertising with Google. Those advertisers that are unable to generate a profit using Google ads often will say things like, "Google is too expensive or too over saturated." However, the truth is that those advertisers are not getting results using Google because they either lack the time, the knowledge or both to properly optimize their campaigns.

For those advertisers with the proper tools and the ability to use them, advertising on Google and specifically Google Shopping for ecommerce retailers can be one of the most profitable marketing channels available. A marketing channel that delivers sales 24/7, 365 days a year.

I have been running paid ads using Google Ads for almost two decades and running Google Shopping ads since even before the inception of paid Google Shopping in 2012. During this time, I have managed hundreds of thousands of dollars in ad spending for my private clients.

Pulling on this experience, what I discovered is that one of the most effective ways to optimize a Google account on an ongoing basis is to let historical data be your guide. Quite simply, this means increasing bids on items that are converting and decreasing bids when items are not.

I'm a big believer in the 80/20 rule as it applies to your Google Shopping ads. I see it true time and time again when I review a retailer's Google Shopping account. The 80/20 rule used with respect to Google Shopping dictates that 20% of products will generate 80% of conversions.

Although this 80/20 rule is common in most Google Ads accounts that I review, unfortunately for many advertisers, what is also typical is having near similar bids across all products in an account or in multiple campaigns.

I want to show you a better way to quickly and effectively optimize your Google Shopping campaigns.

In order to be able to effectively optimize Google Shopping campaigns based on historical data, an account first must segment products into manageable sizes and separate campaigns.

Running a single campaign with 'all products' is not going to allow an advertiser to optimize their bids for best-selling items and, worse than that, will typically waste a ton of money in ad spend.

Having a single campaign with 'all products' is the default of launching a Google Shopping campaign, and sadly, some advertisers never get past this point.

No wonder most retailers are not profitable using Google:>

If this is your situation and you haven't segmented your Google Shopping campaigns, don't despair, but please motivate yourself to act and start segmenting.

I dedicated Chapter 9 to all about it; if you skipped ahead, now would be a good time to review - How Segmenting Google Shopping Campaigns Can Boost Profitability.

Once an account is properly segmented into related campaigns, it will become much easier to run my propriety profitability report along with having the ability to easily optimize your bidding for device, location, time or day of the week.

All these optimizations are helpful for getting the most results and the lowest cost-per-acquisition; however, the most effective way to optimize your campaign relatively quickly is by using my proprietary *Profitability Report*.

How The Profitability Report Works

For Google Search ads, retailers can set automated rules that increase or decrease bids based on conversions or lack of conversions. However, automated rules are not available for Google Shopping ads.

By using my Profitability Report system, advertisers can naturally raise bids on products that convert, while lowering bids for items that are not converting.

In order to effectively run the Profitability Report, you are first going to need to be familiar with how to run reports inside the Google Ads interface as well as some advertising formulas such as ROAS (rate on ad spend).

If you are not familiar with these terms, don't worry, they are all detailed in my free download – T.O.P. Google Profitability Report.

Is the Profitability Report Right for You?

Here is a list of advertisers that could substantially increase their sales with the use of my proprietary Profitability Report within Google Shopping.

Advertisers with over 20 products in Google Shopping who:

1. Do not know what items are driving sales within their Google Shopping campaigns.

2. Are not currently bidding higher for best-selling or bidding lower for items with low conversion rates.

3. Are not adjusting their Shopping product bids at least monthly based on historical data.

4. Do not have a system for monitoring their best-selling and least-selling products.

Do this weekly and you will see your profitability from Google skyrocket as you bid more for items producing profitable conversions and less for product ads that are currently eating your budget.

PROFITABILITY REPORT

Creating the Profitability Report

1. Click on reports icon in top tool bar.

2. Select Predefined Reports > Shopping > Shopping – Item ID.
   ≡ Shopping - Item I

3. This should populate the following key performance indicators (KPIs): Item ID, Clicks, Impressions, CTR, Avg CPC, Costs, Cost/Conv and Conv. Rate.

4. You will then want to add Conversion Value, Campaign and Ad Group. Note, adding a column is done by dragging the desired field from the left menu to the table. It may be necessary to click on the three horizontal lines to display all options.

5. Save As 'Profitability Report'

6. Note, once the repot is saved you can schedule the created report to automatically run so next time it will be available in advance.

Using the Profitability Report

1. Click on reports icon in top tool bar.

2. Download the profitability report for the desired date range (suggestion is weekly).

3. Create a new column for rate on ad spend (ROAS) – conversion value/costs.

4. This is where some discretion comes as far as optimizing. For the accounts that I manage, if the ROAS is between 2 - 5, I raise by 20%; if between 5-10, I raise 35%; if over 10, I raise 50%. For most of my accounts, I use a $5 threshold for costs; however, this can be adjusted depending on the accounts volume.

5. To make it easier, I add a comment field with the action to on the item and highlight with a color – example: green for all items that need to be raised.

6. Next, I sort by poor performing item ids. To do this, sort by cost from largest to smallest.

ROAS Formula

$$ROAS = Conv\ Value/Costs$$

Action

ROAS 2-5 > 20%

ROAS 5-10 > 35%

ROAS over 10 > 50%

Costs over $10 with 0 conversions < 25%

Costs over $5 with 0 – conversions < 15%

7. Set your criteria. For example, in the accounts I manage, I lower bids by 25% on any item that spends over $10 with $0 sales and lower bids by 10% on any item that spends over $5 with $0 sales. Again, I color code the items that need to be decreased in order to easily determine.

8. I then sort the excel sheet by Notes and then Ad Group.

9. You now have an easy to read file where you can make actionable changes.

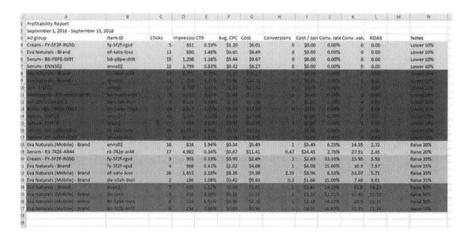

Final Word

Those who say that Google is over-saturated or too expensive to effectively use Google Ads as a highly profitable marketing channel typically do not have a system in place to optimize their Google advertising.

In Google Shopping, what is most likely occurring is that they are bidding too high on products that do not convert and not high enough on products that do have a high probability of leading to a sale.

Now, you also need to look at your website. If you are selling products from a website that, to be relatively nice, looks like crap and doesn't convey confidence in the shopping process, it still may be difficult to convert.

Google Shopping ads should produce higher conversion rates than what organic traffic produces. But, if your organic traffic has a conversion rate of under 1%; for example, there are other factors such as having a poor website, pricing pressures, or a variety of other reasons that may account for the issue.

In this case, even if you produce a Shopping conversion rates double to, let's say, 1.5%, it may be difficult to show a substantial profit using Google ads.

However, for an average website selling products where there is a market to buy them, Google Shopping Ads, when done right, can provide you with a consistent and highly profitable marketing stream.

CHAPTER 13

Mobile Equality – It Almost Is Never Fair, Nor Should It Be So

There are many times that things need to be equal. When you are splitting a sandwich in half for your kids, that should be equal, or when you are balancing your finances, all that should be equal.

However, how much you are bidding for your ads to appear on various devices between desktop, mobile and tablets using paid advertising that should almost NEVER be equal.

It is no secret that mobile has exploded and has come a long way in a short period of time. I distinctly remember attending the Internet Retailer Conference in 2011. The theme of the conference that year was to NOT concentrate your efforts on mobile, but instead concentrate your marketing efforts on social media, especially Facebook and Twitter.

Wow, were they wrong!

Although social marketing is catching up in terms of importance and should not be ignored, there was no doubt with me, then or now, that mobile is a much more important aspect of today's online marketing.

A huge percentage of Google searches have shifted from desktop to mobile, and the percentage of users using mobile devices continues to climb. In fact, Google now reports that over 50% of searches are now performed using mobile devices.

Statistics are helpful, but the real question becomes: what is the appropriate bidding strategy for mobile devices for your company?

The answer depends on your specific company and can be determined in part based on your answers to the following questions:

1. What percentage of your traffic comes from mobile?

2. What is your conversion rate on mobile visitors?

3. Is your site optimized for mobile (how does it look for mobile users)?

4. How are your current campaigns working for mobile including your current ROI and ROAS (how profitable are they)?

These are fundamental questions that each marketer needs to know the answer in order to begin optimizing their paid advertising for mobile.

Fortunately, by having Google Analytics installed along with the historical data available from the Google Ads account, the answers to these questions can be easily attained.

Answering The Questions

The first two questions of what percentage of your traffic is generated from mobile devices along with the conversion rates generated from mobile visitors can be answered at the same time.

In order to view an overview of your traffic, your will want to use Google Analytics. Later, when adjusting bids for individual campaigns, you will review historical data and adjust the bidding within the Google Ads interface.

The first step is to open your Google Analytics account. Hopefully, you already have Google Analytics properly installed as it provides much useful data for measuring the health of your overall website other than the conversions segmented by device.

In the left menu, select 'Audience' then 'Mobile' then 'Overview'. Here you will be able to view your conversion rates based on device – mobile, desktop or tablet.

The numbers typically will appear as the example below:

This is a very typical results for ecommerce retailers. It reveals that almost twice the traffic is coming from mobile devices (4,605 visits in mobile vs. 2,883 visits in desktop).

Looking at this report also reveals that the mobile conversion rate is only about 1/3 of that generated by desktop devices (0.64% - mobile vs 1.81% - desktop).

The report also shows statistics for tablets. Also, very typically for this retailer, tablets have about 1/2 the traffic of desktop and the conversion rates are somewhere between mobile conversion rates and desktop conversion rates at 0.90%.

Now that we have answered the first two questions of what percentage of traffic is coming from mobile and what the conversion rates are for mobile devices, we can look at the question – is your site optimized for mobile?

There are many different ways to optimize your website for mobile. In fact, Google offers free tools such as testing the speed of your website available through Google's developer tools - https://developers.google.com/speed/pagespeed/insights/ (which is very important).

However, I find that the most effective way to see if your website is optimized for mobile is to place test orders for your products using mobile devices. Put yourself through the user experience repeatedly, and you will discover if there are issues that could be lowering your conversion rates.

Ask your employees or family or friends to also test and give you honest feedback of anything they see that may prevent them from ordering using their iPhone or Android. Today, almost everyone has experience online shopping, and you will find this type of feedback provides valuable and actionable insight.

In fact, I recommend personally placing orders using different devices at least on a bi-weekly basis in order to deeply understand your website's checkout experience.

Although most mobile traffic comes from Apple iPhones, make sure you do not ignore other devices. In order to view which devices are generating traffic, again return to Google Analytics.

You are going to go to the left menu again and select 'Audience' then 'Mobile' however, this time, select 'Devices'. This report will display the traffic and conversion rates based on the different type of device – Apple iPhone, Tablet type, Samsung Android type, etc.

Audiences			Acquisition	
User Explorer		Mobile Device Info ?	Users ? ↓	New Users ?
▸ Demographics				
▸ Interests		·	**5,004** % of Total: 23.97% (20,877)	**4,793** % of Total: 24.35% (19,681)
▸ Geo				
▸ Behavior	☐ 1.	Apple iPhone	**2,275** (45.46%)	2,241 (46.76%)
▸ Technology	☐ 2.	Apple iPad	**1,040** (20.78%)	976 (20.36%)
▾ Mobile	☐ 3.	Microsoft Windows RT Tablet	**152** (3.04%)	133 (2.77%)
Overview	☐ 4.	Samsung SM-G960U Galaxy S9	**100** (2.00%)	95 (1.96%)
Devices	☐ 5.	Samsung SM-G950U Galaxy S8	**83** (1.66%)	82 (1.71%)
▸ Cross Device ᴮᴱᵀᴬ	☐ 6.	Samsung SM-G965U Galaxy S9+	**70** (1.40%)	66 (1.38%)
▸ Custom	☐ 7.	Samsung SM-G975U Galaxy S10+	**70** (1.40%)	68 (1.42%)
⚲ Attribution ᴮᴱᵀᴬ	☐ 8.	Samsung SM-N960U Galaxy Note9	**60** (1.20%)	54 (1.13%)
♀ Discover	☐ 9.	Samsung SM-G955U Galaxy S8+	**48** (0.96%)	44 (0.92%)
⚙ Admin	☐ 10.	Samsung SM-N950U Galaxy Note8	**48** (0.96%)	48 (1.00%)

Making Actionable Changes

By viewing historical data within Google Analytics, we are able to discover what our overall traffic and conversion rates are based on device. However, to make actionable changes on our bidding, we need to use the Google Ads interface to review our historical data.

Bid adjustment for devices is available at the account, campaign or ad group level within Google Ads account. If you have a large selection of products, you will discover that conversion rates based on device can vary greatly depending on your product offering. This is another reason that it is critical to subdivide your campaign.

Creating A Device Adjustment Report

1. From the All Campaigns view, click on 'Devices' in the left navigation menu.

145

2. Adjust columns to display the following KPIs: Device, Level, Added to; Bid adj, Ad Group Bid Adj, Impr., Clicks, CTR, Costs, Conversions, Cost/Conv.,

Conv. Rate and Conv Value.

3. Adjust the date to the desired date range (recommended last 30 days).

4. Use the filter button to show only data that has spent more than $5.

5. Download the report and save.

Using the Device Adjustment Report

1. Open the Device Adjustment Report.

2. Create a new column for rate on ad spend (ROAS) – conversion value/costs. With the ROAS include for the total (last row of file).

3. Use the total column's ROAS to create a variance of 50% higher; 25% higher; 25% lower and 50% lower.

Example, assume your average ROAS is 8.9

Multiply 8.9 by 1.5
= 13.35 (50% higher)

Multiple 8.9 by 1.25
= 11.13 (25% higher)

Multiple 8.9 by 0.75
= 6.67 (25% lower)

Multiple 8.9 by 0.50
= 4.45 (50% lower)

ROAS Formula

ROAS =
Conv Value/Costs

Action

ROAS 50% or higher –
increase bid 50%

ROAS 25% to 50% -
increase bid 25%

ROAS 25% to 50%
lower – decrease bid
25%

ROAS 50% or lower –
decrease bids 50%

4. Sort the file by ROAS from high to low.

5. Sort by Bid Adj. column and where there is no current bid adjustments, replace the '- -' with a zero (0).

6. Add a new column named variance. If it is in the 50% range, mark those rows 50%; if in the 25% range, mark 25%; if in the 25% lower range, mark -25%; if in the lower 50% range, mark -50%. Do not add to field where ROAS is between 25% higher or 25% lower than average.

7. For items with no conversions, if there is a spend over $20 – mark variance column with -50%. If spend between $5 – $20, mark variance column -25%.

8. Sort by variance and delete rows where the variance is blank. These Ad Groups already have an optimal bid producing

between a ROAS of between 25% below to 25% above the account average.

9. Create a new bid adjustment column. This is where it gets a bit complicated, but entering the correct formulas is essential and will pay dividends when optimizing your account:

For items where the variance is positive and current bid adj is negative - use the following formula.
(1 * variance) + current bid adjust.
Excel formula = (1*Q127)+E127

For items where the variance is positive and current bid adj is positive - use the following formula.
(current bid adj * variance) + current bid adj
Excel formula = (E331*Q331)+E331

For items where the variance is negative or positive and current bid adj is negative - use the following formula.
(current bid adj * negative variance) + current bid adj
Excel formula = (E122*-Q122)+E122

For items where the variance is negative and current bid adj is positive - use the following formula.
current bid adj + (current bid adj * variance)
Excel formula = E272+(E272*Q272)

For items where there is no current bid adj and variance is positive or negative - use the following formula.
(1*variance)+ current bid adj
Excel formula =(1*Q324)+E324

10. Once you have all of the bid adjustments in place, highlight all negative bid adjustments in red and all positive bid adjustments in green.

11. Sort by campaign, then ad groups. Now you have an actionable file based on historical results!

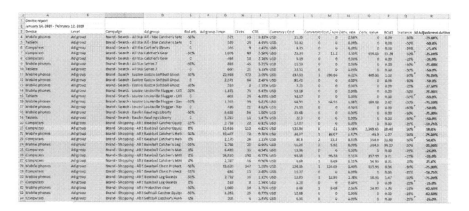

Final Word

Remember when you were daydreaming in math class and wondering when you would ever use advanced math formulas in real life?

Here it is!

We have seen how bidding the same for all devices is a fool's game as all devices do not convert equally.

We also see how creating an actionable file takes work to create. However, I can guarantee that your competitors most likely are not spending the time to effectively and systematically adjust their bids based on device.

By doing the work, you are going to have a huge advantage over your competition and be able to precisely optimize your bids based on what device they are using when coming through paid ads. This process will effectively increase bids where conversions have historically occurred and decrease bids where they have not.

Also remember, to use these advanced techniques, I advise you to first segment your campaigns. For a review on segmenting, review my chapter 8- *How Segmenting Google Shopping Campaigns Can Boost Profitability*.

CHAPTER 14

Increase Your Conversions by Knowing Your Customer's Location

Location, location, location, it is the well-known battle cry of real estate agents, but it just as well could be the battle cry of the savvy online marketer.

Depending on what products you are selling, your conversion rate may differ substantially depending on which part of the country your clients reside.

Imagine this scenario for the scuba diving retailer (I'm not pulling this example from thin air, I previously worked with a scuba diving retailer as a private client a few years ago).

As you can probably imagine, the users searching for scuba diving gear who live near the water - Florida, California, Texas, etc. had higher conversion rates than those not by the water – Nebraska, Iowa, Kansas, etc. Meanwhile, the users searching in high income areas not by the water, New York, Denver, Chicago, etc. were somewhere in between – assuming they were planning their trips.

Therefore, to optimize the account, I used location bidding to bid more for areas by the water with the highest conversions; lowered the bid slightly for areas not by the water but with higher average income and bid substantially lower for areas not by the water with very few conversions.

What Does This Have to Do with You?

I realize you probably don't sell scuba diving gear, but if someone asked you if your CPA (cost-per acquisition) was the same across all states, would you know? Would you know which states are generating your highest conversion rates and at what CPA?

For each campaign?

That's right, if you have followed best-practices and grouped campaigns into similar products, then conversions rates may very well vary by location even within different campaigns.

If your campaigns are not currently optimized by location or you don't know how this is done, then you should read the rest of this chapter.

Below, we will reveal exactly how to dive into your Google Ads account to uncover this data. Once you can identify trends in user behavior based on their location, you can optimize your campaigns based on historical data to increase your profitability.

Accessing Location Data

You can access location data at either the account or campaign level.

In order to access it, you are going to click on 'Location' located in the left-hand menu.

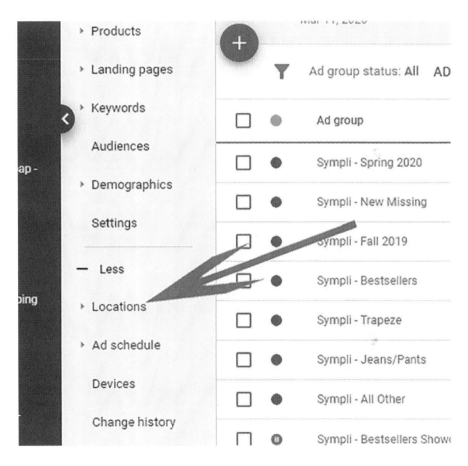

Then, you will click on either 'Geographic report' or 'User Location report' located below the 'Location link.

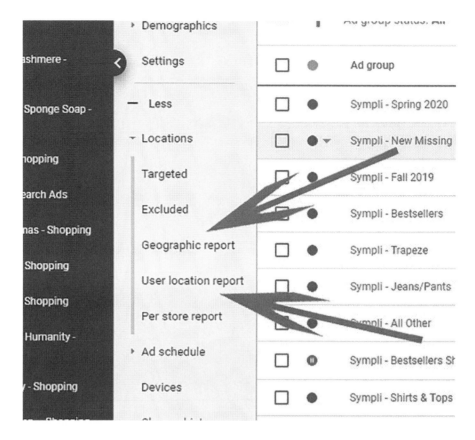

Geographic Report displays the location that triggered your ads to display based on both location as well as area of interest.

User location report displays the location that triggered your ads to display based exclusively on destination.

Which should you use?

If you are advertising a product or service that is specific to a geographical region – example Georgia football shirts, then you may want to use the geographic report to optimize bids as you would want to be able to subdivide data by both actual location as well as area of interest.

However, if you are selling an item with no geographic ties – example children's tricycles, then best-practices would suggest using the user location report to subdivide and optimize on your data.

For the example below, I will use the User location report.

Once you click on the User location report, the report displays at the top level which is for country.

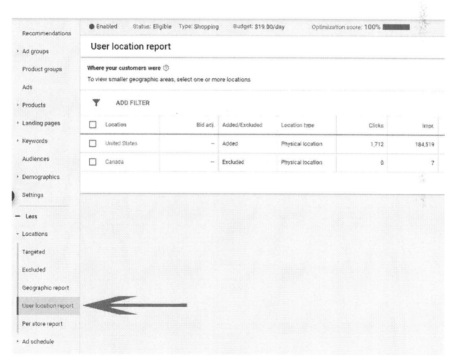

If you then click on the country, options will open including region, state, region, congressional district, county, municipality, city, postal code, airport, borough, city region, neighborhood university and district.

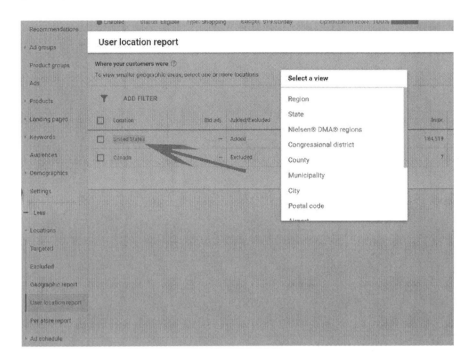

For my private clients, I generally will subsegment by state or even by city if there are substantial conversions to warrant.

Once you open the report, basics columns will display including clicks, impressions, CTR, Average CPC, Cost, Conversions, Cost/Cov and Value/Conv. You are also able to add additional KPIs (key performance indicators) by clicking on the column button on the report. You can also export the data into an excel file if that makes the data easier for you to work with.

Once you have identified some trends and are ready to either increase or decrease bids, you will click the checkbox next to the field you wish to adjust; select the edit button and choose Add targets and set bid adjustment.

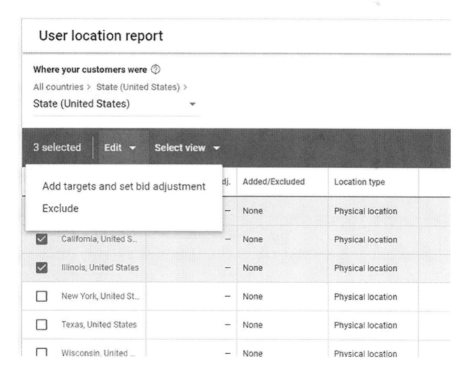

Proprietary Best Practices for Adjusting Bids

Now that you know how to extract your data and how to either increase or decrease bids, the important question becomes when to make the bid adjustments and how much to adjust the bids.

This is up to the individual advertisers of course, but here are the guidelines that I use for the majority of my private clients.

First, I calculate the ROAS – Conversion Value / Costs. This can be done by exporting the data into Excel and adding a column with the formula above to automatically calculate ROAS.

For items with traffic over a certain threshold (say 200 clicks over the last 30 days), I change the bids based on the following results:

ROAS 2-5 – Increase bids 10%

ROAS 5-10 – Increase bids 15%

ROAS 10-24 – Increase bids 25%

ROAS over 25 – Increase bids 40%

For categories, with certain number of clicks (say 100) and 0 conversions, I would look at lowering bids.

100 – 150 clicks with 0 conversions – Decrease bids 10%

150 – 200 clicks with 0 conversions – Decrease bids 15%

Over 200 clicks with 0 conversions – Decrease bids 25%

Final Word

If you are not reviewing the locations from which your conversions are being generated, you are most likely wasting ad spend AND not capitalizing on the ability to increase profitable conversions.

By setting up a schedule of when you review these locations, you can systematically increase or decrease your bids for areas that either historically either do or do not convert.

It is important to note: for this method to be effective, you will need to be sure that you are properly tracking your conversions.

However, if your account tracking is properly installed, you will soon discover how effectively adjusting bids based on conversions can boost your overall account profitability.

CHAPTER 15

Increase Your Conversions by Knowing When Your Customers Shop

We have previously discussed optimizing your bids based on how your customers shop your website (device) and where your customers shop from (location). This chapter will dive into the third part of the triangle – when your customers shop and optimizing bids based on that past data.

One mistake many advertisers make is thinking that their customers shop at random times throughout the day. For your products, this very well may be true, and I'm not writing this to argue whether, in fact, it is or isn't true.

There is no need to argue the fact. Assuming you are properly tracking your conversions, Google provides all of the data you need to review your historical data and determine whether there is a trend with the time or the day your customers have historically purchased more or less from your website.

What Are Ad Schedules?

In order to optimize by the day of the week or time of the day, we must first create an ad schedule. Creating an ad schedule in Google allows us to view when customers are shopping (traffic) and converting (sales) throughout the day and throughout the week.

Ad schedules will also allow us to adjust bids based on certain times of the day or days of the week (this will come later in this article).

Ad schedules are, by default, formatted and running in your account from day one of using Google Ads. However, they are not shown and are set to 'All day' by default. This means that your ads are eligible to appear at the same bid at any time during the day or day of the week.

By customizing a custom ad schedule, we will soon discover if there is a pattern to our sales and use that data to adjust our bids based on this historical data.

Important Notes Regarding Ad Schedule

A couple of important notes for creating ad schedules:

First, when creating an ad schedule, it will operate using the time zone that you set when creating your account.

Therefore, if your account is set to central time, for example, and you create an ad schedule for 9am – 5pm, this will adjust your ads for 10am – 6pm EST and 7am – 3pm PST. Unfortunately, as of now, there is no way to change the time based on customer location.

Second, ad schedules can only be created at the campaign level.

Third, there is a limit of six ad schedules per day per campaign.

Creating an Ad Schedule

Before you can make any changes to your bids using an ad schedule, you need to first gather data. In order to start gathering data, you will need to create an ad schedule.

To create your first ad schedule, follow these steps:

1. Navigate to the campaign for which you wish to create the ad schedule.

2. Click on the blue pencil icon or the Edit Ad Schedule button.

3. Make your selection for specific days and times. (Again, remember that the ad schedule you set is based on your account's time zone).

4. Click the Save button. You should see your created ad schedule shown on the Ad schedule page.

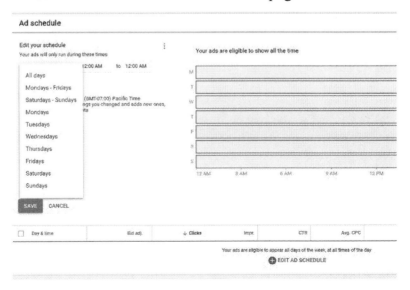

When creating an ad schedule, there are multiple options enabling advertisers to choose how they would like to segment the day and days of the week.

For Professional Service advertisers, it is semi-common to use an ad schedule to only serve ads while customer service is open.

However, for those of us that advertise for eCommerce stores that are open 24/7, it is more important to adjust bids rather than wanting to exclude the time that ads are shown.

Therefore, typically for my private clients, I will set up an initial ad schedule that looks like this:

> All Days: 12AM – 5AM
>
> All Days: 5AM – 5PM
>
> All Days: 5PM – 8PM
>
> All Days: 8PM – 12AM

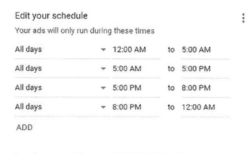

In the example above, I'm assuming the account has been set to PST. This means that the times ads are running are going to be different depending on the customer's time zone.

Example 12AM – 5AM PST is going to be 3AM – 8AM EST. However, the important thing to note is that I segmented out the times into four groups – before the typical office day, during the typically office day, in the evening and late at night.

If I'm working on an account in a different time zone that serves ads throughout the US, I will adjust the schedule based on the time zone of the account.

By segmenting in this way, I'm able to determine the shopping pattern for accounts I manage based on these four segments.

Once you are finished creating the ad schedule and save you should see your ad schedule save (however, with no data).

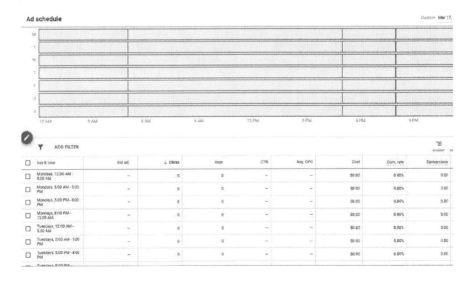

Making Bid Adjustments in Ad Schedules

Once your ad schedule has been running for some time (I like to at least look at a month), you may want to adjust bids for certain times of the day or certain days of the week.

When managing accounts for private clients, I typically review multiple campaigns; exporting the data and adjusting bids based on changes to the variance – similar to changing mobile bidding as described in a previous chapter - *Mobile Equality – It Almost Is Never Fair, Nor Should It Be So.*

For now, we are just going to look at the steps for adjusting a bid within an ad schedule.

1. Navigate to the campaign you wish to adjust the bid for the ad schedule.

2. Click on the Ad Schedule link in the left-hand menu.

3. Select the checkbox next to the ad schedule you wish to adjust (if making multiple changes) and click edit. If making a single change, you can click on the pencil icon next to the Bid Adj column.

4. Make your change and save.

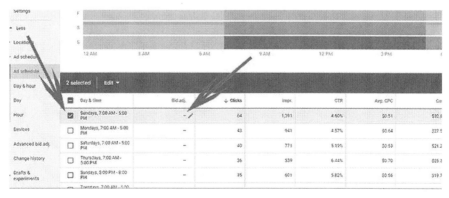

By adjusting bids, you can increase or decrease your bids based on the ad schedule you have created.

Important note, that increasing bids for ad schedules will be in addition to other adjustments that are currently running in your campaigns, including mobile bid adjustments and location bid adjustments.

Assume you are bidding $1 for an item and are increasing mobile bids by 25%; adding a 25% increase for a location and now you are adding a 25% increase for time of day.

By doing a little math we can determine that we now could be bidding a maximum of $1.95. (1 X 1.25 x 1.25 x 1.25 = 1.95). Down the road when reviewing campaigns, if you see your average CPC higher than the set bid, this is often the reason.

Final Word

Bid adjustments are a great way to optimize sales for eCommerce advertisers who can accurately determine a large discrepancy in either day of week or time of day when their customers are shopping.

If you can identify a distinct pattern to your customers behaviors, by adjusting bids to match those behaviors you can increase sales and profitability within your campaigns.

However, when optimizing ad schedules, it is important to note that your data needs to be significantly relevant in order to ensure patterns are viable and not random. You will want to make sure you have at least a month of data before making any changes, and when you first make changes, you will want to monitor closely for either negative or positive affects to your advertising.

CHAPTER 16

Using Audiences to Increase Conversions

There is a lot of trust that you need to convey to customers when making an initial sale.

Does a customer trust your products? Does a customer trust your price? Does your customer trust your shipping times? Does a customer trust that your website is secure?

However, for a user who has previously placed an order and become a customer, those trust factors have been established. The only barrier to having the customer place their next order is the customer again needing your product(s) and the customer being able to find your product(s) again.

By utilizing Google's tracking system, advertisers can keep tabs on past buyers and create a list of those buyers in what is called an audience.

By using audience lists to increase their bidding, advertisers can help ensure that past buyers are more likely to find their products the next time they are searching Google.

Not only can advertisers create an 'audience' of past buyers, but also an audience of past website visitors who did not buy or an audience of past visitors who exited after visited your checkout page or an audience of past visitors who stayed over two minutes on any page and didn't buy.

I think you get the point.

With Google's tracking tag, advertisers have practically limitless ways to segment website visitors based on the way they interacted with their website and can group them into different audiences.

In addition, audiences are not limited to website visitors and how they have previously interacted with your business. Advertisers also are invited to tap into Google's research into its users and how Google has segmented those users by specific interest, demographics, habits and how they are searching, even for those who have never visited their website.

If you want to get crazy, and if you find an audience that converts, why wouldn't you, you can also add audiences similar to your created audiences, again filled with potential customers who have never visited your website.

Although Google audiences can be used in shopping, search, display and video, this article discuss how to use them and the benefits of using them exclusively for shopping campaigns.

Creating Audiences in Google Analytics

The first step is that you need to have already properly installed Google Analytics and linked Google Analytics to your Google Ads account.

Although, we don't go into details on the importance of properly installing Google Analytics in this article, Google Analytics and the data it provides is crucial in terms of proper tracking and optimizing of your Google Ads account.

Once you are inside of Google Analytics, you will want to navigate to the 'Admin' view. To access the 'Admin' view click on the 'Admin' link located in the very bottom of the left navigation bar.

The Admin view is divided into 3 sections: Account, Property and View. For our task of creating audiences, we will be using 'Audience Definitions' located within the Property section.

Once you click on the Audience Definitions, a new window will open that displays all previously created audiences and a big, red New Audience button. In order to edit existing audiences, click on the audience name. In order to create a new audience, click on the red 'New Audience' button.

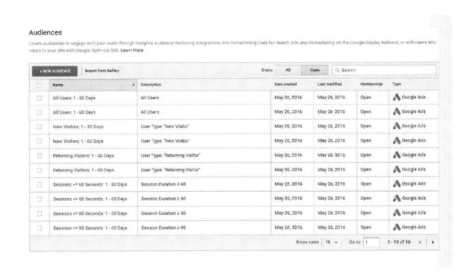

Creating a new audience is almost limitless in what you can create. However, it is segmented into 3 main sections: Audience Source, Audience Definition and Audience Destination.

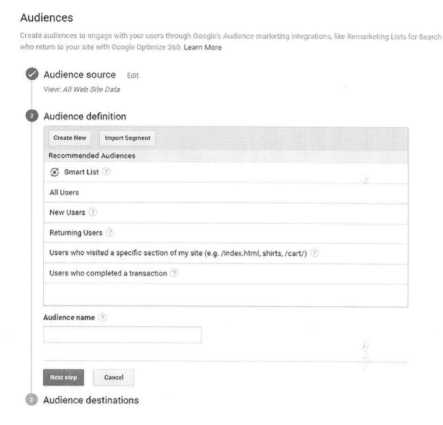

Audience Source

The audience source is where advertisers add the first party data source to their account. Most advertisers are going to have only one 'View' in their Analytics account, so this field will pre-populate.

Audience Definition

Audience Definition is where advertisers can define their audiences. Google recommends a few pre-populated definitions such as All Users, New Users, Returning Users, Users who visited a specific section of my site and users who completed a transaction.

By clicking one of the recommendations, you can then customize the recommendation and change the membership duration (how long the user stays in your defined audience).

To customize a Google recommended audience type, click on the audience type and then the pencil icon.

This will open a new window where advertisers can overlay their own criteria. Criteria that can be used is also virtually unlimited. It includes Demographics, Technology, Behavior, Date of First Session, Traffic Sources, Enhanced Ecommerce, Conditions and Sequences.

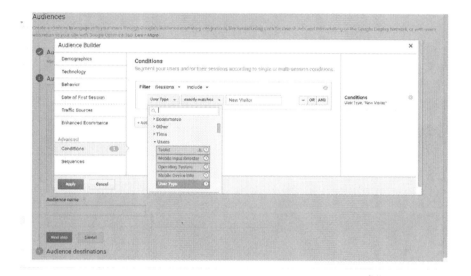

Once you define your conditions and you click the blue 'Apply' button, the only thing left in this section is to name your audience.

Audience Destination

The Audience Destination section lets Google Analytics know where you want to apply your created list. Since we are going to use the audience to bolster our shopping campaigns, we are going to link the audience destination to our Google Ads account.

To do this, simply click on the 'Add destination' button and select the correct Google Ads account. If the account is not already linked,

you will have to first connect your Google Ads account to your
Google Analytics account.

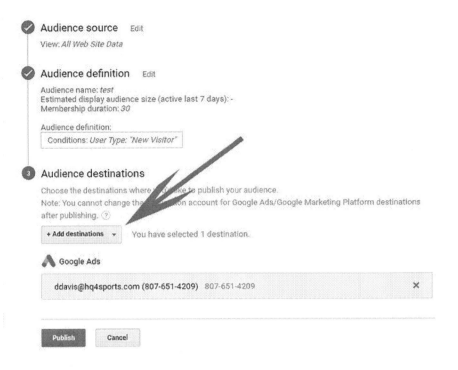

Click Publish, and you are done. You are ready to now start using
your campaign to adjust bids within your Google Ads Account.

Using Your New Audience

Before you can start using audiences, the audience is going to have
to grow large enough before Google will allow you to use it.
Currently, the list for targeting search/shopping campaigns must be
over 1,000 in the last 30 days before it is eligible for use.

Depending on your traffic, it will of course vary how long it takes before the list is eligible. However, once the list has grown to the required size, your goal will be to adjust bids for audiences where purchase is more likely.

For shopping campaigns, audience bids can be added and adjusted at either the campaign or the ad group level. Note, if you add audiences at the campaign level it will affect all ad groups inside that campaign. However, if you add audiences at the ad group level it will ONLY affect that one ad group.

Adding an Audience

To add an audience, navigate to the campaign or ad group where you want to add the audience and click on the 'Audiences' link in the left-hand menu.

Then, you will click on the blue pencil icon, which will open a new window.

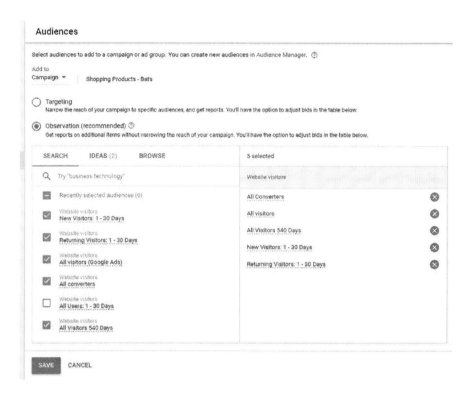

In this window, you can confirm where you want to add the audience, which audience to add and how you want to apply the audience.

Observation – This setting ads an audience but continues serving eligible ads as normal.

Targeting – This setting will override the campaign or ad group targeting and ONLY serve eligible ads to the selected audience.

If you suddenly see a dramatic drop in your ads being served, you probably selected the wrong targeting type. Observation is going to be typically used unless you are running a specific campaign such as retargeting visitors.

Once you enter your new audiences, you can adjust the bids for specific audiences by clicking on the pencil icon in the 'Bid adj.' column.

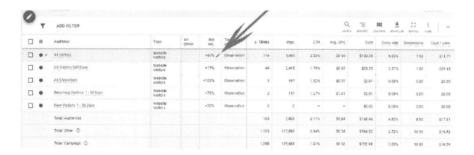

Here you also will want to ensure that you have set your Targeting to Observation in order to continue serving ads to all users as well as your defined audiences.

Typically, advertisers will find a lower CPA (cost per acquisition) for audience list. Therefore, it makes sense to bid more on those customers.

As your account and your campaigns continue to compile more data, you will be able to optimize bids for past website visitors in order to increase conversions.

Final Word

The first sale is always the hardest to make. For a customer to push that 'Confirm Order' button, they need to trust your website and trust your products.

Once the customer has completed that first order and you have successfully fulfilled that order, if everything goes right, you now should have a happy customer.

The barrier to having a happy customer place a second order, third order or fourth order is far lower.

That is why email marketing to your customer list is so powerful. However, your email marketing might now reach them the exact time they are searching for your product(s) in Google.

By creating audiences and increasing bids for those audiences, you can help ensure your past customers or past website visitors find your products more easily and quickly during their search.

The eCommerce average of a happy customer making a 2nd purchase is 30%; the average of a third sale is 35%; the average of a fourth sale and beyond is 90%. Therefore, doesn't it make sense to do everything you can to ensure customers continue to make repeat sales?

Creating and implementing audiences, when used properly, is an effective way to increase the lifetime value of a customer and it should be a piece of your online Google Ads strategy.

SECTION 4

Automating Google

Recently, the wife, children and I took a trip back to the Midwest to visit family. The plane ride from Los Angeles to Omaha, Nebraska is only about 3 hours, which isn't too daunting even with a 10-year old and a 4-year old.

However, due to all Boeing 737 type aircraft currently being grounded, there are very few direct flights.

Nowhere is it more evident today of how automated our world is becoming than at the airport. In order just to start the check-in process, you must enter your own information at a kiosk which then prints out a baggage tag that you must attach to your own bag to move to the next automated step.

In fact, when checking into the flight, the only human interaction I had (outside of being frisked by an overly friendly gentlemen in a FAA security suit) was handing my already prepped luggage to someone whose job it was to put it on a handling rack that was sorted by flight.

Once aboard the airplane, I began thinking about all the automations that were going on in the background in order to fly the airplane and how these automations were responsible for welfare of all of us passengers.

After all, the whole reason that the Boeing 737 was grounded was due to some automated software failures.

I actually wasn't as nervous as it sounds as I had some interesting insight from my brother who is a commercial airline pilot. He had told me that the 737 accidents weren't because of a software failure, but instead, they were caused based on how the pilots reacted to the software failures.

Also, he added, international commercial pilots are trained to solely rely on automated systems while American commercial pilots are trained first how to fly manually and then to rely on automated systems.

I'm not an expert on anything remotely connected with flying a plane, but that explanation did seem to make sense to me.

I know in my world of optimizing online advertising, the same sort of principle applies.

Google keeps introducing new automated ways to optimize your Google Ads.

For those that rely solely on these automated bidding strategies, it is very possible they may crash and burn (at least with their ROI!).

And although most advertisers typically find better results from properly managed MANUAL Google Ads, automated bid strategies are an option especially for those that don't want to 'train' on how to optimize their accounts themselves.

This section features the automated bid strategies that are available from Google within Google Ads.

Even for those of you that are fully trained manually optimizing Google Ads from a time when no automations where available (like 2 years ago), I suggest you discover what options Google now offers.

For my private clients, I'm always testing the newest releases from Google in some fashion.

After all, it is all about profits and increasing your ROI, no matter if it is manual or automated.

Just remember, there is no Federal Aviation Administration regulating and protecting the automations of your online advertising, and it will be up to you to see how you react if something goes wrong using automated bid strategies :>

Let's get started.

CHAPTER 17

Is Using Google Smart Shopping Campaigns Smart for Retailers?

Google has introduced a new way for advertisers to manage their Shopping campaigns, aptly named 'Smart Shopping campaign'. However, who are Smart Shopping campaigns designed for and what advertisers would benefit from implementing "Smart" shopping campaigns as opposed to Standard Shopping campaigns?

So, what is Google's Smart Shopping Campaigns?

Google promotes their Smart Shopping campaigns as a way for advertisers to simplify their campaign management while maximizing conversion values and expanding their reach.

Campaigns that use the Smart Shopping setting are eligible to appear across Google's Search Network, Display Network, YouTube and Gmail.

A Smart Shopping campaign will take priority over Standard Shopping campaigns. This means that if a product is listed in a Smart Shopping campaign as well as a Standard Shopping campaign, the

Smart Shopping campaign is the campaign that Google will use to serve a retailer's ads.

How do Smart Shopping campaigns work?

Google uses an advertiser's existing product feed as submitted to Google Merchant Center and combines eligible products with Google's machine learning to serve ads across their list of networks - Google's Search Network, Display Network, YouTube and Gmail.

A merchant determines their budget, and Google automatically tests ads for different combinations of products and keyword searches, promising to deliver retailers the maximum amount of conversion value for their ad spend.

What is required for Google Smart campaigns?

Before an advertiser can setup Smart Shopping campaign, they will need to make sure they comply with some initial setup procedures that include:

1. Conversion tracking will need to be configured along with transaction-specific values.

2. The website will also need to add a global site tag to the website and have a remarketing list with a minimum of 100 active users.

3. Finally, advertisers will need to meet all requirements for Google Shopping campaigns as well as follow the standard Google Shopping ad policies.

How can you tell if Google Smart campaign is working?

If an advertiser wants to test using a Google Smart shopping campaign, it is advisable to allow the campaign at least 2-3 weeks for Google's algorithm to work. Don't turn off the new campaign within a day or two, give Google time to test their Smart Shopping algorithm to see if Google is providing desired results before evaluating performance.

Second, advertisers will want to make sure the budget and products are comparable to historic data from past Standard Shopping campaigns when evaluating.

Note, if using a ROAS goal, initially advertisers may see a decline in the number of clicks and impressions they are receiving. This is normal as Google tries to deliver conversions within the settings of the campaign's profitability goals.

So, what is the upside of using Google's Smart Shopping campaigns?

Using Smart Shopping campaigns can provide retailers with extended reach beyond the Google Search Network. With Smart Shopping campaigns also delivering ads to the Display Network, YouTube and Gmail, retailers may find additional sales beyond the Google Search Network.

Also, for retailers with limited time or knowledge to properly manage their campaigns, Google Smart Shopping campaigns are an ideal way to simply define what profitability they would like to achieve without the time-consuming task of optimizing for negative keywords, bids, device bidding and the many other factors that go into running a successful Google Shopping campaign.

What is the downside of using Google's Smart Shopping campaigns?

Advertisers do not have control over where or how many times their product ads are appearing across different networks. Google DOES NOT provide data on what networks or keywords are driving conversions.

Google's Smart Shopping algorithm supposedly works by providing maximum conversion value, but Google does not provide specifics on the how, where, what and why. Instead, they ask for retailers to give Google the blind trust that Google will spend the advertiser's money efficiently.

This is kind of like putting the fox in charge of the hen house, as Google charges again based on the bids that they are creating for the advertiser's product listings without the advertiser having any control over specific bids or even being able to review where ads are showing or at what bids.

Additionally, advertisers are not allowed to opt out of certain networks, making Google Smart campaigns and all or nothing proposition as far as where ads are eligible for display.

So, what is the bottom line?

Advertisers, especially those with limited-time or knowledge of how Google Shopping works, may want to test to see if running Smart

Shopping campaigns are more profitable than running Standard Shopping campaigns.

Being able to show ads across different networks may be profitable for advertisers. However, be aware that you are giving up quite a bit of control and trusting that Google will be providing 'maximum conversion value' beyond what can be achieved running Standard Shopping campaigns.

Final Word

For my private clients, I would advise that, typically, a well-run Standard Shopping campaign should deliver results and insights into their business that are not available with Smart Shopping campaigns.

With the proper use of negative keywords and the ongoing optimization of past results, the upside of being able to control where product ads are eligible to appear outweighs the promises of letting Google handle your account and letting Google control your bids and placements while trying to maximize your profits.

However, like anything, there is no or, at least (if you keep budgets low), little harm in testing. I have seen results vary based on product line, and there is the possibility of an upside with increased exposure across all Google networks.

CHAPTER 18

Google Smart Shopping Campaigns – What You Need to Realize

A few weeks back, I was contacted by a former private client. When last we worked together, he had been running an eCommerce health supplement business and had just sold his interest.

Now, a couple of years later, he was back at it with an all new e-commerce health supplement business.

He was confused and looking for help to figure out what was going on with his account. He had submitted a feed to Google Merchant Center using the free Shopify app (he had a Shopify store) and had an agency set up a Google Shopping campaign but wasn't receiving any traffic.

What Was Going On?

After looking at his merchant center account and his Google Ads account, I quickly diagnosed his issue.

First, the "free" feed app linking Shopify and Merchant Center is a major issue for any retailer wishing to customize their feed, especially a company that retails health supplements, whose products are on the fringe of Google policy.

Have you ever heard the saying, 'You get what you pay for'?

Although there is a fee involved, most eCommerce retailers would be better advised to use a 3rd party data optimization company to format and have the ability to customize their data before sending their feed to Google Merchant Center.

The cost of data optimization companies typically ranges anywhere from $10 a month to $100s a month, but what you will get back in conversion rates based on the ability to optimize Google Shopping accounts with any volume at all will far outweigh the cost.

Using a data optimization company gives you the ability to add custom labels (the lifeblood of proper segmentation with Google Shopping) as well as the ability to tweak titles and descriptions so they don't appear exactly as they do on the webpage.

For health vitamins, some ingredients are an absolute policy violation and will cause disapprovals just by having the name of a particular ingredient listed on a product page.

However, some ingredient names are not absolute, but will cause a disapproval if they are listed in the submitted title or description; although they will not trigger a red flag by simply being listed on the landing page.

Although health supplements are an extreme example, most retailers could benefit incrementally by being able to optimize their product titles in their data feed in terms of improving CTR and relevancy for keywords. Using a data optimization company allows retail advertisers to quickly make those tweaks without having to change the title or description on their actual product pages.

Here is the bottom line:

Using a free option to submit feeds, regardless of what eCommerce platform you are using, is generally a bad idea. In order to run a successful Google Shopping campaign, you need to first have a strategic plan with your data feed. This will give you the ability to segment your Shopping campaigns and effectively be able to optimize bids based on history.

For information on properly optimizing Shopping campaigns based on historical data, review Chapter 12 - *Effectively Optimize Google Shopping Based on Your Past History, Nothing More.*

Google Smart Campaigns

The second issue this retailer was facing was using a Google 'Smart' Shopping campaign to send his products with a bid strategy of 'Maximize Conversions'.

Google promotes their Smart Shopping campaigns as a way for advertisers to simplify their campaign management while maximizing conversion values and expanding their reach.

Campaigns that use the Smart Shopping setting are eligible to appear across Google's Search Network, Display Network, YouTube and Gmail. However, you are leaving all the control up to Google.

In addition, the 'Maximize Conversion' strategy has Google attempting to only serve ads when ads have the best chance to convert.

Sound pretty good, right?

How the Google Smart Campaigns Typically Perform …

Google uses an advertiser's existing product feed as submitted to Google Merchant Center and combines eligible products with Google's machine learning to serve ads across their list of networks – Google's Search Network, Display Network, YouTube and Gmail.

A merchant then determines their budget and bid strategy and Google automatically tests ads for different combinations of products and keyword searches, promising to deliver retailers the maximum amount of conversion value for their ad spend.

A major issue with Google Smart Campaigns is that retailers have no knowledge of where their ads are appearing or for what keywords or at what cost.

An advertiser, fortunately, can access how many clicks they receive and at what costs. For this retailer, his average cost-per-click was over $6! This was astronomical as his bids hovered around $1.10 a couple of years ago for basically the same product line.

The issue for not being able to view data on which keywords you are appearing is a major drawback. For this particular eCommerce retailer, Google wasn't matching items and searches very well. Even for a search for an exact product name, his products were not displaying in Google Shopping.

Now how does Google Smart Campaigns sound?

Recommendations on What to Do

The first thing I would recommend for this advertiser is to make a change from using Shopify's free data feed app to a paid 3rd party data optimization company.

Currently using Shopify's free app, this retailer had approximately 25% of their products being disapproved in Merchant Center. This could be much lower.

By using the Diagnostics links in Merchant Center and using the ability of a 3rd party data optimization company to adjust the title and description, this merchant should be able to significantly reduce their disapprovals.

For more information, see chapter 2 - *There Can Be No Google Shopping Without a Google Merchant Account.*

Next, there are some options with how the Google Ads account is setup. The first and easiest solution would be to change the bidding strategy goal. Smart Shopping campaigns are always set to 'Maximize Conversions'; however, advertisers have the ability to change the ROAS (return on ad spend) goal. By lowering the ROAS goal, the retailer could potentially gain more clicks if there have been enough conversions to optimize.

However, I would highly recommend that this merchant split out their campaign into multiple campaigns. It would make sense to split out the campaigns by brands, at least for the top-selling brands.

To effectively split out the account into different campaigns, it will require a plan when submitting the data feed to ensure that everything is properly formatted to allow for segmentation.

Once the account is divided into different brand-oriented campaigns, the customer can test continuing using Smart campaigns or make the switch to manual campaigns.

By starting to manage and optimize in a 'standard campaign' retailers are able to access data on exactly which products are driving traffic, converting, spending and for what keywords. This allows optimization of the products as well as the ability to use advanced strategies such as the Positive Keyword Strategy – 'Positive Keywords – A Better Way to Control Unwanted Searches' Chapter 24.

Final Word

This company, incredibly, paid an agency a few hundred bucks to set up this campaign! Besides being ill-advised, the work to set up this campaign took five minutes max and cost the advertiser not only a setup fee, but an ongoing monthly retainer. This demonstrates the importance of knowing how Google Ads work regardless of whether or not a retailer decides to manage their account in-house or outsource to a SEM agency.

I am an advocate of testing. With so many types of ads, bidding strategies and now new automated bidding strategies available, what works best for one account may not work the best for all accounts.

A few months back, Google started showing an 'Optimization Score' on every campaign which includes a score between 1-100% as well as recommendations. The recommendations are a fantastic way to make sure every campaign has key conversion elements such as ad extensions (for search ads), keyword targeting, the use of audiences, etc.

However, the only way the Optimization Score goes to a 100% is if a campaign uses Google's Smart Shopping, an automated bidding strategy.

Utilizing Smart campaigns, in fact, most of the time, is not the best option for advertisers, but you may want to test it.

However, before changing any Shopping campaigns to Google Smart Shopping campaigns, make sure you are aware of the downfalls. You must realize that 'Smart' Campaigns will mean that Google handles your bids and PLA ad placements and know that you will be flying blind with Google behind the wheel.

CHAPTER 19

Google's Automated Bidding Strategies

Since the 1980's the concept of 'Artificial Intelligence' has been debated on its merits of either advancing society or being the eventual end of mankind.

I'm not willing or ready to join that debate nor is this the proper forum to do so, but what I will discuss is Google's semi-new automated bidding strategies.

For those Google advertisers with the time and the knowledge to properly segment and optimize their Google Ads campaigns, typically you will generate better results and gain important insights not available when you manually segment, optimize and actively manage your campaigns.

However, like anything, you won't know for sure if optimizing campaigns manually is more effective than Google's automated bidding strategies if you don't test. I recommend and am always testing different bidding strategies for my private clients, and I suggest that you do the same.

I'm not proposing that you test your entire account, but a subset of your account that may not be performing well or at least is not your most essential account during your busiest time of year makes an excellent candidate for testing:>

A quick note when testing is that you will want to understand the bidding strategies before running any test, so pay attention to the rest of this chapter and discover which strategy may be the right fit for you and your advertising goals.

And for those of you who lack the time or knowledge to properly optimize your campaigns (if you are reading this chapter), know that using a Google automated bidding strategy is going to far outperform doing nothing, so know your options.

Automated Bidding Strategies – What They Are

In general, the purpose of Google's automated bidding strategies is to automatically set bid values in order to maximize the likelihood that a click on your ad will result in a conversion.

In order to calculate the likelihood of conversion, Google uses past historical data including search terms, click through rates, device, operating system, time of day, etc. to either increase or decrease bids in real-time based on the selected bidding strategy.

For automated bid strategies to be effective, advertisers will first need to ensure that they have properly configured their conversion tracking and then that they have established conversion history and know their campaign goals.

Automatic bid strategies can be changed easily through the settings link at either the campaign, ad group or keyword level depending on the strategy.

By using automated bidding strategies, advertisers are addressing two problems that can be commonly found within manually optimized campaigns:

1. Ensuring that bids are set high enough to compete with other qualified advertisers.

2. Ensuring that bids are not set too high, which can result in ads being shown on too loosely relevant of user queries where there is little likelihood of purchase.

Note, we are discussing the automated bidding strategies, which are not to be confused with Google's Smart Shopping Campaigns.

Google's Smart Shopping Campaigns.

We covered Google Smart Shopping Campaigns in detail a few chapters back in *Google Smart Shopping Campaigns – What You Need to Realize*.

Types of Automated Bidding Strategies

Google offers six different automated bidding strategies – Target CPA, Target ROAS, Maximize Clicks, Maximize Conversions, Maximize Conversion Value and Target Impressions Share.

All six of these campaigns are available for use in Search campaigns, while only two automated bid strategies are currently available for Shopping campaigns – Target ROAS and Maximize Clicks.

My feeling is that soon all the automated bid strategies will become available in Shopping campaigns. Therefore, even if your Google Ads account is predominantly Shopping campaigns, it is advisable to know the difference between the automated bidding strategies and to even test how they work and their effectiveness within your Search campaigns.

TARGET CPA

The lingo – CPA – Stands for Cost per Acquisition. In other words, what is the average amount it costs you to generate a sale?

The strategy - Google automatically will adjust an advertiser's bid in order to get as many conversions possible at the advertiser's selected cost per acquisition goal.

Where it is available – campaign and ad group levels.

When to use – This strategy works best when you already have an established CPA with over 30 conversions in the last 30 days. You can use this strategy to either lower your CPA or to maximize conversions by setting the Target CPA slightly higher than your last 30-day average. Note, this strategy will remove any location/device bid adjustments that are currently active.

TARGET ROAS

The lingo – ROAS – Stands for Return on Ad Spend. To calculate ROAS, divide gross revenue by ad spend.

The strategy – Google automatically will adjust an advertiser's bid in order to get as many conversions possible at the advertiser's selected ROAS goal.

Where it is available – campaign, ad group and keywords levels. (Shopping & Search Campaigns).

When to use - This strategy works best when you already have an established ROAS with over 50 conversions in the last 30 days. In addition, this strategy makes sense only when conversions have different conversion values.

MAXIMIZE CLICKS

The lingo – A click is calculated each time a user clicks on your ad and is directed to your website.

The strategy - Google automatically will adjust an advertiser's bid in order to get as many visitors as possible to your website within your set budget.

Where it is available – campaign, ad group & keyword levels. (Shopping & Search Campaigns).

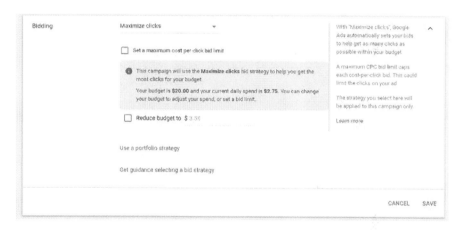

When to use – You have a historical high conversion rate and you would like as many visitors as possible sent to your website.

MAXIMIZE CONVERSIONS

The lingo – A conversion is what the advertiser defines as their end goal. For eCommerce retailers, this is typically a product purchase. For others, a conversion could be as simple as joining a mailing list.

The strategy - Google automatically will adjust an advertiser's bid in order to get as many conversions within the set budget.

Where it is available – campaign level.

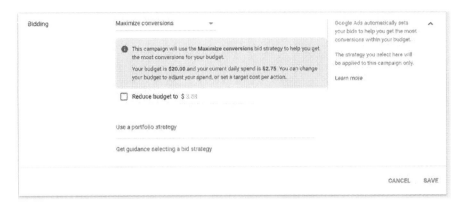

When to use – You have a reasonably large budget and wish to generate as many conversions as possible.

MAXIMIZE CONVERSION VALUE

The lingo – The conversion value is the total value of all conversions.

The strategy - Google automatically will adjust an advertiser's bid in order to gain the maximum conversion value within the set budget.

Where it is available – campaign level.

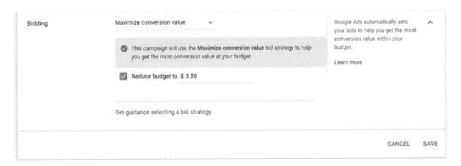

When to use – You have a reasonably large budget with conversions of drastically different conversion values.

TARGET IMPRESSION SHARE

The lingo – Target impression share is the percentage of time your ads appear at the top of the page.

The strategy - Google automatically will adjust an advertiser's bid in order to generate ad placement at the top of the page as often as possible within the set budget.

Where it is available – campaign level.

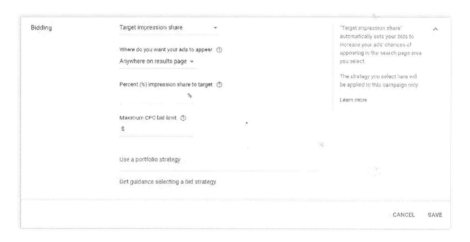

When to use – You have a reasonably well performing conversion rate with a reasonably large budget but are struggling with how often your ads appear at the top of the page.

Final Word

You probably have heard the phrase 'All Roads Lead to Rome'?

This is true when optimizing your Google campaigns, as there are many ways to achieve your goal of conversions. However, although there are many ways to achieve conversions, some will perform better than others.

By better, does that mean lowering your cost-per-acquisition or increasing the number of conversions?

The key metrics that matter are going to depend on your goals as an advertiser and how you wish to best utilize Google in your advertising.

However, whether manually optimizing or using one of Google's automated strategies, it will require testing to discover which strategy performs the best based on your advertising goals.

CHAPTER 20

Google Shopping Actions – Changing the Landscape

There is no doubt that Amazon has changed the game when it comes to online Shopping. In fact, you may say Amazon has changed the game, changed the field and removed the goal post if you would like a football reference!

I recall while speaking a Small Business Conference that preceded the Internet Retailer Conference in Chicago five years ago that one panelist offered a presentation on the growth potential of Amazon.

At that time, Google accounted for about 80% of all shopping related searches, while Amazon was just a part of the other 20%. Today, Amazon has flipped this number and accounts for more than 50% of all online Shopping searches.

The question for Amazon's competitors, including Google, becomes how Amazon created their meteoric rise into becoming today's Shopping behemoth and how do its competitors (including Google) incorporate some of those online strategies into their own strategies?

Amazon revolutionized easy online ordering in 1999 with their patent protected one-click ordering method. Typically, when ordering from a website, whether the first time or the tenth time, shoppers would have to enter their shipping information, then their billing information and then their payment information.

With Amazon's one-click ordering, they revolutionized that process. Once a customer entered their information once, the customer could return and place their next order in a matter of seconds simply by clicking on a single button.

Amazon's patent on one-click ordering expired in September of 2017, opening the door for others, including Google the ability to adopt this technology.

What Led to Amazon's Growth?

Not only does Amazon sell products themselves, but approximately 50% of products for sale on Amazon are offered by 3rd party merchants. These merchants hold and store their own products and ship their own products when they receive an order through Amazon.

For these merchants, Amazon works strictly as the middleman, taking a percentage of the sale (somewhere in the 15% range) for the service of allowing merchants to list their products on the Amazon platform.

In addition, merchants have the option to bid to have their products shown higher on the page for specific searches on Amazon. This works in the same manner as Google where Amazon conducts a real time auction and combines advertiser's bid with a product relevancy to determine where to place advertised products on a page for select customer searches.

For Amazon, charging advertisers a fee per click, which is how Google has worked for years, is in addition to their commission fees for selling a product.

In addition, Amazon even offers merchants the option of having Amazon hold, store and ship their products (of course for an additional fee on top of what they are already taking for selling the product and for bidding to place the product higher on the page).

The best part (for Amazon at least) is that this system is a great, no-risk way for Amazon to discover what products are selling well. If a product is selling really well, Amazon can then approach the manufacturer directly and start offering the high-selling product directly, of course, with no advertising costs, often times at a much lower price that is negotiated through the manufacturer.

Enter Google Shopping Actions

We see how Amazon has become more like Google with allowing merchants to advertise their products with a real-time auction/pay-per-click format. However, Google introduced their Shopping Actions to adopt some of the systems that has made Amazon so successful.

Google already had the Shopping infrastructure in place through Google Shopping, which has been running since 2012. However, Google Shopping has always consisted of individual merchants listing their products and, starting in 2012, paying each time one of their products was clicked.

In Google Shopping, Google charges a fee based on an advertiser's bid using a real-time auction and quality score when shoppers click on a product ad. Once an ad is clicked, Google Shoppers are directed to the advertiser's website. The checkout process and any other interactions once a user clicks on a shopping ad takes place on the advertiser's website.

With Shopping Actions, checkout as well as other transactions such as returns and exchanges are handled directly by Google. This allows Google to offer one-click ordering as well as to be able to dictate terms for shipping and returns.

When an order is received through Shopping Actions, Google sends the details of the order to the advertiser of what product(s) to ship and the customer address to deliver the order. Once Google receives payment from the customer, they send the funds for the order less a transaction fee of approximately 15% directly to the merchant's bank account.

The Benefits of Listing in Google's Shopping Actions

There are reasons for advertisers to be excited to list their products in Shopping Actions. Being able to reach Google's shopping audience and only paying commission is exciting for those retailers who struggle with profitability of running Shopping Ads or have a limited budget to test their Shopping Ads.

Here are other reasons advertisers should be excited:

1. Pay per sale fee structure – No more pay per click.

2. List products on additional platforms. Products listed through Shopping Actions are eligible to appear on Google.com, Google Shopping AND Google Assistant. (Currently, Google reports having over 500 million Google Assistant enabled devices).

3. Increase conversion rates. Similar to Amazon, customers can purchase from multiple merchants at the same time using Shopping Actions. Plus, if they are repeat customers, they can order quickly using one-click ordering. Conversion rates are also increased due to the trust factor of Google compared to other websites where a potential shopper may be wary of the security of placing an order.

4. Larger Orders - Google has reported a 30% increase in basket size for early merchants who participated in Shopping Actions.

5. Build your email list – Unlike Amazon, Google will prompt shoppers to signup for its merchant's email list, plus merchants receive all of the customer's data, making it easy to build your email list.

6. No competition from the marketplace – Also, unlike Amazon, Google has no intent in going into the business of

shelving and fulfilling products. Therefore, if a merchant has a product that is selling well, they don't have to worry about Google swooping in and competing with them by directly advertising and fulfilling the same product line.

Note, image taken from Google's official blog.

The Drawbacks of Listing Products in Google's Shopping Actions

1. Determining when products appear. With Shopping Actions, there are no bids. Google alone decides when and where to display a merchant's products. Although Google does provide some insight within Google Merchant Center about which products are serving and which are not, this blind system can be frustrating for merchants who are not having products served often.

2. Bidding against your own Shopping Ads. For those merchants already doing well, the fear is that listing products within Shopping Actions will drive up the amount of their

bids in Google Shopping. Although there is no data on this, Google has ensured that this is not the case. Although, to be safe, individual merchants are advised to test.

3. Pay-per-sale model. While paying per sale is great for those advertisers with high average cost per acquisition, some advertisers with well optimized campaigns and a high ROI (return on investment) may find the approximate 15% commission a significant increase.

4. Integrating orders received from Shopping Actions. When an order is received through Shopping Actions, the order comes through within the advertiser's Google Merchant Center account. Making sure the order is integrated into the advertiser's fulfillment process can sometimes present a challenge.

Eligibility to Sell in Shopping Actions

When Shopping Actions first launched, it was exclusively open only to big box retailers – Target, Walmart, Ulta Beauty, etc. By partnering exclusively with big box retailers, Google tested and discovered how grouping the shopping experience would translate within the customer experience.

The results were almost 100% positive and are highlighted in the benefits of listing with Google Shopping section of this article. These benefits include higher conversion rates and higher overall cart value for individual merchants.

Today, Shopping Actions is available for all sized retailers as long as advertisers apply and abide by the following Google's requirements:

1. Must have a valid Google Merchant Center account.
2. Must ship orders within 4 business days.
3. Must have a USA based fulfillment and returns operation.
4. Must have a USA based bank account.
5. Must meet all of the customer service and returns standards.
6. Must fully comply with all Shopping Actions policies.
7. Must fully comply with all Shopping Ads policies.

Getting Products Listing in Shopping Actions

The first step to selling within Shopping Actions is to apply to the program. To apply – https://www.google.com/retail/solutions/shopping-actions/ and click the blue Get Started button.

Before you can go live with products using Shopping Actions, you will need to provide the following product and business information. This information will be entered within your Google Merchant Center Account.

1. Products – Advertisers are required to upload a new product feed of products that they want listed in Shopping Actions or they can add the Shopping Actions destination to their existing feed.

2. Business information – The location headquarters or where the business is registered.

3. Branding – Logos and store colors that will appear with your marketing materials.

4. Tax – Your sales tax setup of what locations you collect taxes and at what rate.

5. Shipping – The shipping rates that a customer will be charged when they purchase your listed products.

6. Return settings – The business default return setting and return address.

7. Taxpayer information – An advertiser's taxpayer id used for US federal income taxes.

8. Banking information – The bank account information of where you would like money from Shopping Actions sales transferred.

9. ID Verification – Ask for verification from the banking information step.

10. User roles – Define and restrict access for different users to Shopping Actions.

Most of these steps are self-explanatory, and you can access them by clicking on the 'Shopping Actions setup' located under the tools icon (wrench) in the upper right corner.

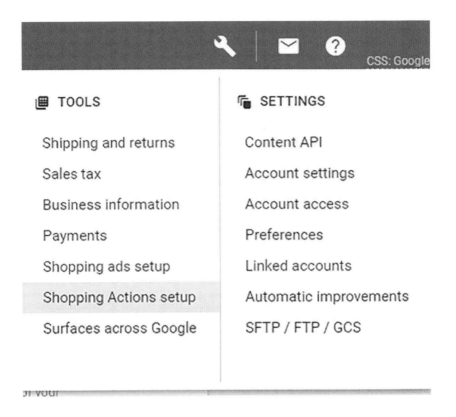

The step that will require a bit more setup is the Products step. The easiest option is for an advertiser to add all their products in an existing feed to Shopping Actions.

To do this"

1. Click on an existing feed. (Access feeds by clicking on 'Products' in the left navigation and then click on 'Feeds').

2. Click on the existing feed name you wish to use to submit products to Shopping Actions.

3. Navigate to 'Settings' – Click on the country, and you can add and remove destinations.

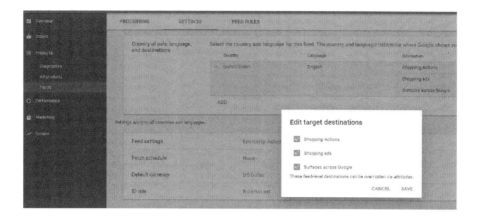

Advertisers also have the option of creating a new feed exclusively for Shopping Actions and then adjust the destinations above for the new feed as well as existing feed in order to control which products are served on which platform.

Once you have submitted your products to Shopping Actions, within 24 hours, you will start to see a Shopping Actions graph populate the home dashboard of your Merchant Center Account.

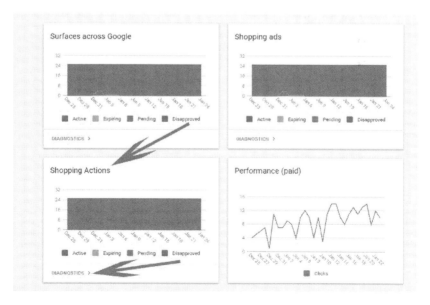

213

From there, you can check on the health of your product listings by clicking on the 'Diagnostics' link located under the graph.

Once you have begun running products through Shopping Actions, beyond the Shopping Actions graph on your dashboard, Google provides other tools to manage your Shopping Action listings within your Merchant Center account.

Orders Link

Located in the left-hand navigation menu, the orders link only appears for merchants who have been approved to have their products appear within Google's Shopping Actions.

By clicking on this link, merchants will find orders from Google Shopping Actions that are Pending, Pending Delivery and All Orders (history). The Orders link also contains historical return data again for Google Shopping Action orders only.

Products Link

Also located in the left menu, this link has always appeared within your account. However, once you have products running for Shopping Actions, you can access individual products or sort products by submitted channel.

These insights are NOT available in the Google Ads interface and is one reason that reviewing the Merchant Center Account on a regular basis is highly recommended.

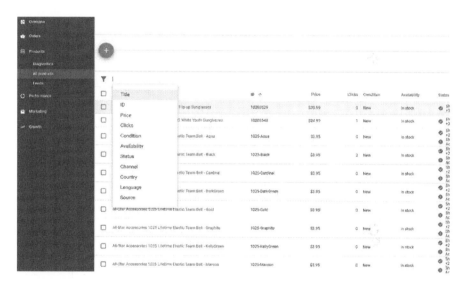

Marketing

Under the 'Marketing' link also located in the left-navigation bar is a link for 'Promotions'.

215

Here, advertisers can boost exposure and conversions by running various promotions for products within Google Shopping as well as products in Shopping Actions.

Growth

Finally, under the 'Growth' link, advertisers will find a new link 'Shopping Actions insights'.

Shopping Actions Insights provides advertisers with sortable data on how their products are performing with Shopping Actions including percentage of buy box wins, top products, competitor's products and more.

Since there is no bidding to control placement in Shopping Actions, this is where advertisers should look to discover why products may or may not be performing at expectations.

Final Word

Google Shopping Actions has the potential to be a game changer for not only Google Shopping ads, but for online Shopping in general. Google remains by far the platform with the largest online footprint, and now that they have incorporated a model proven by Amazon to provide exponential growth, it would be wise for retailers to start planning on where it makes sense to list their products inside of Shopping Actions.

How listing products in Shopping Actions will affect Google Shopping and advertisers who use Google Shopping is still unknown. Preliminary studies that have been released from Google have shown very positive results for advertisers who list products in both Google Shopping and Shopping Actions.

That is why savvy retailers are working quickly to be among the first to start listing their products inside the Shopping Actions platform in order to discover for themselves how Shopping Actions can increase their sales.

SECTION 5

Advanced Techniques

Google recently sent me one of their bicycles as a reward for my agency status. It is a very colorful bike, decked out in Google colors with multiple Google stickers. In fact, you may have seen a picture of a similar bike online as it is one of the same type of bikes that are used throughout the Google campus in Mountain View.

And although I haven't ridden a bicycle in probably thirty years, I decided that it would be a good idea to take my 10-year old son on a bike riding day trip.

I researched the best place in the Pasadena, California area for beginners to bike ride, for my benefit, and found a popular bike path around JPL (Jet Propulsion Laboratories), the place they work on Space Shuttles and such.

During the bike ride, I'm happy to report that I never fell (I guess it is true that once you learn how to ride a bike you never forget) which was good; I also never saw any space shuttles; which was disappointing:). Besides walking a bit funny the next day, it was a great afternoon and a much-needed break from the busy e-commerce marketing season.

When you are so entrenched in what you are doing, sometimes it is important to take a step back to gain some perspective. Hopefully, those of you engulfed in optimizing your online advertising can pencil this in once and awhile as well.

I recently was having a conversation about perspective and the overall health of his Google account with a member of my 'The Academy of Internet Marketing,' and he asked me how he could become more proficient optimizing his Google Ads account.

Like many eCommerce business owners, he was currently managing his Google Ads account exclusively using the Google Ads interface and had never heard of the Google Ads Editor.

This conversation led me to writing the chapters within this section, which of course I put together in my head during the bike ride:>

This section details some of the most advanced techniques in optimizing your Google Shopping campaigns, including use of the Google Ads Editor, using Supplemental Feeds in Google Merchant Center and exploring a concept known as Positive Keywords.

Used in conjunction, these techniques and processes will help you become more proficient and enable your Google campaigns to be substantially more profitable.

CHAPTER 21

Google Ads Editor – The Difference Between Mastering & Simply Being Proficient

How do you determine the difference between a master and simply being proficient when it comes to managing Google ads?

For me, what constitutes a real master, regardless of subject, are these three things: knowledge; efficiency and quantity output.

Sound right?

Although a proficient user can have all the knowledge on Google ads regarding how it all works and the most effective methods to optimize an account without using the Google Editor, these users will never be able to match the efficiency and quantity output of someone who relies on the Google Editor for making large-scale account changes.

What Is the Google Ads Editor?

Google Ads Editor is a free downloadable application for managing your Google Ads account. Once installed, you can download your account or accounts and make changes to the account within the Google Ads Editor. The changes that you make within the Google Editor are stored 'offline' until you 'Post' the changes, at which time they are uploaded back into your Google Ads account where they are immediately implemented live.

The Google Ads Editor has been designed to be easy to understand and will work even when you are not connected to the Internet.

A powerful resource for those wanting to improve their efficiency managing Google Ads, the Google Editor allows advertisers to quickly make changes in a fraction of the time it takes compared to making the same changes using the Google Ads interface.

Given the capabilities of using the Google Ads Editor, why is it then that more advertisers do not incorporate doing their work within the Editor?

My thought is that those advertisers that are not using the Google Ads Editor simply do not understand its capability or how using the Google Ads Editor will make managing their Google campaigns a whole lot more proficient.

In order to remedy this lack of understanding, I have listed the top time saving tasks that can be performed using the Google Ads Editor. There are many other ways to incorporate the Ads Editor into your optimizing of Google ads, but these should be enough to show you some of what can be achieved.

My Favorite Ways to Use the Google Ads Editor

1. Copy/Cut & Paste

Although there is limited copy and paste function within the Google Ads interface, the process is cumbersome and slow to perform. For example, if you want to copy a search ad between ad groups, you must go to the ad (click copy under the more button); navigate to the ad group you wish to copy; go to the 'Ads & extensions' section of the ad group; click the more button and paste the ad.

If you are very quick, this process can be done in about 1-2 minutes.

If you want to copy an ad in the Ads Editor, you left click the mouse (click copy), click on where you want to copy the ad, left click your mouse (click paste).

If you are slow, this process can be done in about 3-5 seconds!

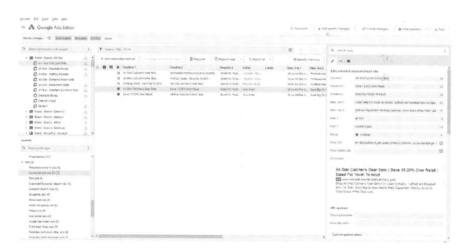

Being able to copy and paste is not limited to ads or even to Search campaigns. Whether modifying your Search, Shopping or Display campaigns, the Google Ads Editor can quickly copy almost anything from one campaign to another including ads, ad extensions, product groups, keywords, settings, audiences, placements and more.

In fact, you can even copy and paste entire campaigns or move ad groups from one campaign to another!

Needless to say, the ability to copy/cut and paste can be a huge time saver when you need to copy or move elements within your account.

2. Bulk Changes

The Google Ads interface is extremely limited when making changes. Advertisers are limited to changes of one at a time or, if very proficient, making multiple identical changes to items within the same ad group (such as keyword bidding).

The Google Editor, in contrast, allows advertisers to use bulk edits to quickly make changes to multiple campaigns simultaneously.

The bulk editing tool allows you to search and replace text, move items, and undo or redo changes across multiple campaigns in a fraction of the time it would take using the Google Ads interface.

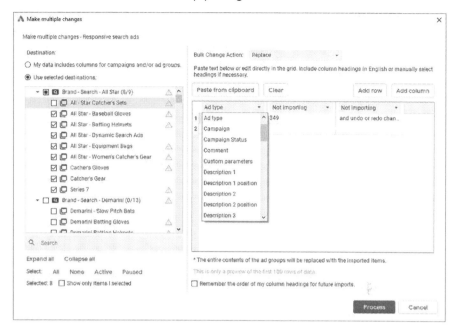

3. Import/Export

If you or someone on your team is more comfortable working making changes in Excel rather than in the Google Editor, no problem. The Google Editor allows you to export data, make changes within Excel and then reupload changes into the editor.

Once you reupload the changes, you can review all changes before approving them and sending them live to your Ads account.

Whether using Excel or the Google Editor to make changes, one thing is for certain – both are a whole lot faster than making changes directly within the Google Ads interface.

4. Find & Replace Text

Using the find and replace text is geared toward working with Search campaigns. This feature allows an advertiser to quickly change text throughout ads.

During the holidays, I found the find and replace tool particularly useful when working on private client accounts, as I would change promotions and details fairly regularly.

Example, you want to change a sale from the 40% you were running during Black Friday to 20% for the rest of the holidays.

If you are using the Google Ads interface, you will need to navigate to each ad and manually make the change at either the ad group or campaign level. Depending on how many ads you are running within how many different campaigns or ad groups, this type of change could take between minutes and hours.

If you are using the Google Ads Editor, you simply use the Find & Replace tool, and the process takes a minute or two regardless of how many ads you are changing!

5. The Ability to Work Offline

With the Google Ads interface, in order to be able to make changes, you need to be connected to the Internet.

With the Google Ads Editor, this is not the case.

And although typically most of us are not spending our days flying through the country on private jets without internet, occasionally this feature does come in handy. You never know when you may be unable to connect to the Internet, but still have changes to make to your Google Ads.

A few weeks back, due to some winds here in Southern California, my Internet was out of commission most of the day during the holiday season. If I did all my optimizing exclusively in the Google Ads interface, I would have been dead in the water.

However, since I work so much in the Google Ads Editor, I was able to work in my private client accounts that had data downloaded, make changes and then upload them into their Google Ads accounts when the Internet was restored.

Final Word

Just because you have always done something a certain way, doesn't necessarily mean it is the most efficient way of doing it.

I, myself, get into this trap of when I have been doing something for so long and it is working fairly well that it is difficult to evolve or even to search if there is a better way.

I was recently at a marketing event, and I was speaking to an individual who coincidentally also ran a Search Engine Marketing company managing private clients. When we spoke about the subject of maximizing time and using the Google Ads Editor, he said, 'I don't need the Editor, I do just fine making my changes directly within the Google Ads interface'.

Although you can work exclusively inside the Google Ads interface (as many advertisers do), using the Google Editor is going to make you much more efficient and increase your quantity output.

The top ways that I have listed above are some of the more popular ways of using the Google Ads Editor, but in no way is it an exhaustive list.

The Google Ads Editor can be used to make any type of change where you are currently changing using the Google Ads Interface, and if you are making more than one change, probably much quicker.

If you aren't currently using the Google Ads Editor, I encourage you to start exploring what is possible and making it an essential tool in your Google Ads management.

Afterall, by become proficient in using the Google Ads Editor, you will be a step closer to becoming a true master in the realm of Google advertising. Well, maybe not a true master, but at least a whole lot more efficient!

CHAPTER 22

Using Supplemental Feeds in Google Merchant Center

Most often, one of the least understood pieces of advertising using Google Shopping is the continuous updating of product data to Google Merchant Center.

Far too often, I have found when reviewing a retailer's Google Ads account, they set up the Merchant Center, linked it to their Google Ads account, and then never or almost never looked at it again. These accounts are often riddled with product disapprovals and inaccurate information.

Although your bidding optimizations are going to take place inside your Google Ads interface, it is critical to keep the data in your Merchant Center up to date. In addition to being accurate, there are tools that savvy Google advertisers use to effectively managing product data.

One of my favorite tools that I use for my private clients is the use of supplemental feeds.

Getting Started Using Merchant Center

Before you can begin advertising using Google Shopping, you need to first properly configure your Google Merchant Center.

For those new to Google Shopping, properly configuring your Merchant Center includes verifying and claiming your store, setting up tax and shipping information and, of course, submitting products.

For a complete review of all the initial steps along with the ongoing reviewing of errors and disapprovals that are sure to happen once you have submitted your products, review the chapter back at the start of the book – Chapter 2 - *There Can Be No Google Shopping Without A Google Merchant Account.*

However, this chapter is written for those who are already running an approved product feed and wish to customize the feed without making changes to the original feed.

If that doesn't quite make sense, no worries. I am about to explain.

Merchant Center Feeds

When uploading your products into Google Merchant Center, you will use the feed section of your Merchant Center account. This section is split into two sections: Primary Feeds and Supplemental Feeds.

The Primary Feed section is where you send the primary feed. The primary feed contains all the data that advertisers use to list and optimize their Google Shopping campaigns formatted into a delivery method that Google accepts.

There are quite a few options for an advertiser when submitting their primary feed.

First, you need to select your country of sale, then the language and finally the destination of where you want your product ads to be eligible for display. The options include Display ads, Shopping ads, Shopping Actions (when activated) and Surfaces across Google.

Next, you name your primary feed and select how you are going to provide the feed to Google.

Options for providing the data to Google include:

1. Using Google Sheets – Merchants create a Google Sheet to hold the data and manually update the sheet as needed.

2. Schedule a Fetch – Merchants host the feed on their own server and schedule a regular time for Google to fetch the feed from that location.

3. Upload – (the most commonly used) – Merchants typically using a 3rd party data optimization company to automate and format the data along with scheduling a regular send.

4. Content API – (the second most commonly used) – Also typically done through a 3rd party data optimization company. This method transfers the data through an API connection directly into merchant center.

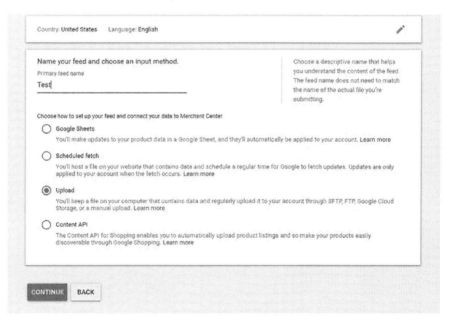

Once you decide on how to get the data to Google, you then need to name the feed and create the initial feed. Some of the settings such as the Default Currency setting will need to be properly specified in order to have the feed approved by Google.

Supplemental Feeds

Once your primary feed is up and running with products being approved, advertisers may feel the need to update information for some of the products in the feed without updating the entire primary feed.

If that doesn't quite make sense, again, no worries. I am about to explain.

For the example below, I am going to show using a supplemental feed to exclude some of the products from being eligible to appear in Google Shopping ads.

Besides being able to exclude items, you can update products using a Supplemental feed for any of the over 50 fields supported by Google Merchant Center.

Supplemental feeds are particularly useful to merchants with thousands of products that are being submitted when they only want to edit a subset of those products. Using a Supplemental feed allows information on a large feed to be overwritten with data in a smaller, easy to manage Supplemental feed file.

One of the ways I use supplemental feeds for my private clients is to exclude a small subset of products from being eligible to appear in one of the four supported shopping channels – Display ads, Shopping ads, Shopping Actions (when activated) or Surfaces across Google.

Other times, a Supplemental feed may be useful when it is not possible to map custom labels for some reason inside a primary feed or, for that matter, any of the other 50 supported fields that need to be changed for a subset of the primary feed.

In this example, I'm going to use a supplemental feed to make some products ineligible to appear within Shopping ads using a Google Sheet.

Creating a Supplemental Feed

The first step is inside Merchant Center to navigate to Products, then Feeds and click on the blue 'Add Supplemental Feed' link.

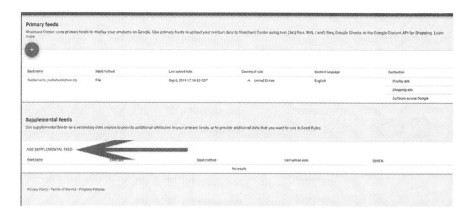

You will then name the feed and select the method for which you would like to submit the data to Google Merchant Center. For this example, I'm going to use Google Sheets.

Google Sheets is like Excel; however, instead of storing the file on your computer, it is stored under Google's cloud storage. Google sheets, therefore, do not take up any storage room, and best of all,

Google sheets are absolutely free to create, use and modify. A Google sheet simply attaches to the same Google account that you use when accessing your Google Ads Account.

In order to create a Google Sheet, you first will want to name your Supplemental feed with a name that helps you recognize the purpose of the feed and then choose how you would like to deliver the data to Google.

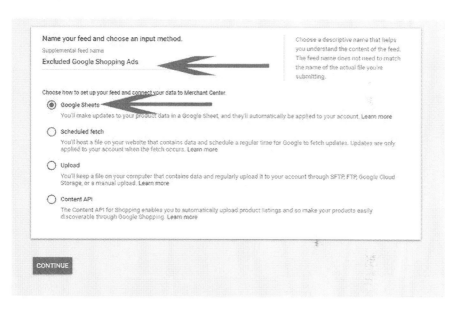

Then, you will select whether you want to generate a new Google sheet or select an existing Google sheet.

Since I am creating from scratch, I'm going to select to generate new Google sheet and click on continue.

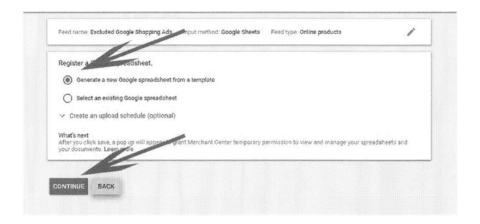

You will then want to select the primary feed that you will want to override data in with the new supplemental feed and select continue.

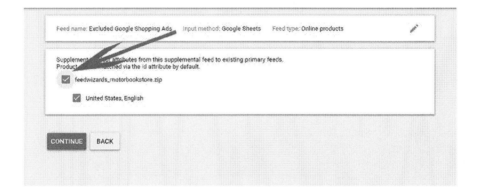

Google will then automatically create your supplemental feed along with a link to open the feed.

Once you open the Google sheet using the blue 'Open' link under in the Input method, the Google sheet will open, and you can manually add data to the file.

When adding data, you will want the first row to be the header row. This row should contain id in the first column (this is what Google will use to match the data in your supplemental feed with the data in the primary feed). The next columns will be the header for the supported fields that you want to override in the primary feed using the new supplemental feed.

For this example, I am using Excluded_destination in order to tell Google that certain items should not be eligible to appear inside Shopping Ads.

Note, in this example, I'm overriding only one field, excluded_destination, but you can override multiple fields at the same time using a supplemental feed. In order to do so, you need to add additional columns, where the header row contains the field you wish to override with the data underneath.

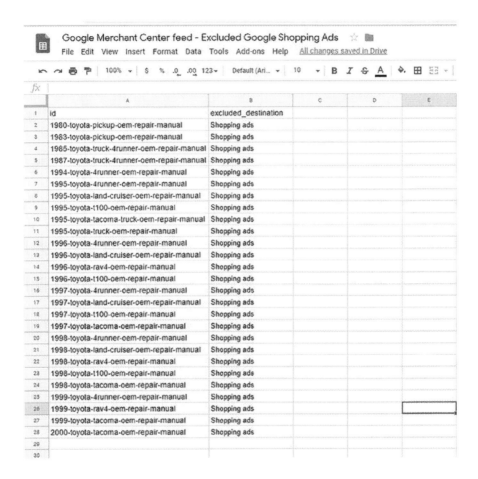

After the Google sheet is saved for the Supplemental feed to take effect, you are going to have to go back to your feeds and click on the Supplemental feed you just created.

Once opened, you will need to click on the 'Fetch Now' link in the upper right.

Once you click the Fetch Now link, Google will import your data and override product data in the original primary feed. Give the feed a few minutes to populate and you should see how many records were successfully populated.

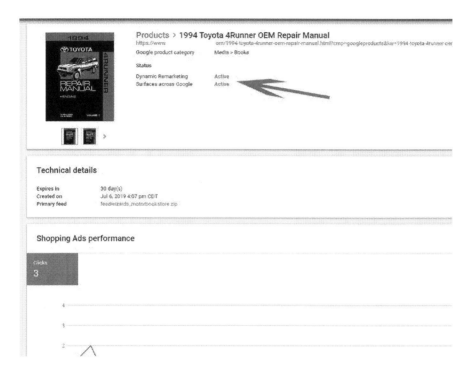

As you can see above, all 27 items that we added were successfully populated!

Checking That Everything Is Working

In order to check to see if the Supplemental feed has taken affect, you will want to click on 'All products' link in the left tool bar, and then you can filter by one of the ids in your new Supplemental feed.

If you click on the item, all the details for this item as stored in Google Merchant Center will display.

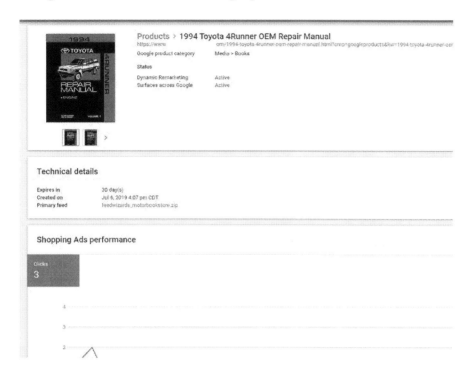

For the purpose of our example, we can see right near the top that the item no longer is appearing on Shopping ads. However, if you changed other fields in the primary feed, you will need to scroll down on the page to see how different fields are now being displayed.

That is it. Congratulations, you now have another highly effective tool for being able to quickly manage the data in your Google Merchant Center!

Final Word

Knowing how your Google Merchant Center pulls in product data is essential to gaining a huge leg up on your competition. Although all the bidding is done within your Google Ads interface, only products that are approved in your Merchant Center will become eligible to appear in your Google Shopping campaigns.

If you are not checking your Google Merchant Center often, you could be doing yourself a real disservice in terms of not monitoring new disapprovals and other issues that will inevitably arise within Merchant Center.

Providing strategically formatted data to Google Merchant Center makes it much easier to control product listings and allows for the best chance for success using Google Shopping.

And now that you know how to quickly control a subset of your products using a Supplemental feed, you have an effective way to manage your products including showing which products are and are not eligible to appear within different channels.

CHAPTER 23

Knowing Your Priority Settings

Google allows campaigns to be configured using different priority settings of low, medium or high. By default, a campaign's priority level is set to low; however, along with bids, priority settings, when you know how to use them, can be a powerful tool in optimizing your Google Ads campaigns.

A more advanced concept, I have found by reviewing hundreds of Google Ads accounts that the usage of the priority settings is one of the key indicators of the skill level of the person managing an account. The proper use of priority settings is one technique that separates the novice from the expert in terms of Google Ads advertising.

What are Google's Priority Settings?

When a product ad is contained in multiple campaigns, the priority level directs Google on which campaign to pull the product ad from regardless of the amount bid.

This can be a bit confusing, so I will provide a further example, but first a quick summary of how Google Shopping determines when to display an advertiser's product ad for a user query, aka user search.

Google Shopping ads do not contain keywords. Instead, Google matches the text in an advertiser's product title and description and best matches to keyword searches using their algorithm that strives to provide the most relevant Shopping results to its users.

Now, if an advertiser has a product ad that is contained within more than one campaign, Google will use whichever product has a higher bid to determine which product ad to display for a matching user search. Since there are no keywords used, and the titles and descriptions would be the same for a duplicate product ad, the only difference that Google has is what the bid is set to when deciding from which campaign an advertiser would like their product ad pulled.

Again, this is only relevant when a product is listed in multiple Google Ads campaigns.

By using Priority Settings, an advertiser can override the bid hierarchy. This allows an advertiser to communicate with Google from which campaign they would like a product ad pulled when their product ad is contained within multiple campaigns.

Let me break it down further.

A product ad contained in a Google Ads campaign set at either 'Medium' or 'High' priority with a bid of only $0.01 would be served (when a user's keyword search matches) instead of the same product contained in a different campaign with a bid of $10, if that campaign has a 'Low' priority. This is in spite the fact that the bid on the product ad in the low priority campaign has a bid 1,000% higher that the bid in the medium or high priority campaign.

I know this is a bit confusing.

I'm going to first cover where to set the priority level and then I'll provide a quick example of how I use priority levels for my private clients, which should clarify how priority levels work as well as how you can use them.

The next chapter, Positive Keywords - A Better Way To Control Unwanted Searches, will go into even further detail on how priority levels can be used to control the quality of search terms.

Configuring Priority Levels

Setting priority levels can be done when first creating a new campaign, or the priority level can be changed on an existing campaign.

When creating a new campaign, an advertiser will first set the campaign type to Shopping and the campaign subtype to a 'Standard' Shopping campaign (note, priority levels are not applicable for Smart Shopping campaigns).

On the next page, an advertiser will name their campaign, set their bids and budgets, set targeting and set their campaign priority of either Low (default), Medium or High.

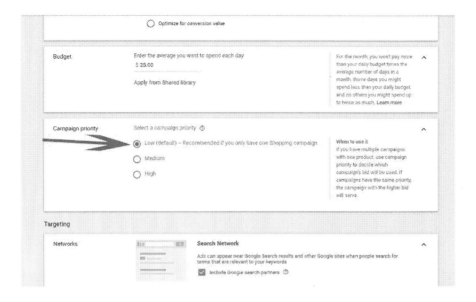

For an existing campaign, an advertiser can change their Priority settings by simply clicking on the campaign name and selecting the 'Settings' link in the left-hand menu.

Using Priority Settings

Now that you know what priority settings are and how to define and change them in your Google Ads campaigns, the next logical question that you may have is when and why would an advertiser use priority settings?

I use priority settings for many of my private clients with a technique called positive keywords.

Here is how it works:

I set a product group containing many related products typically products grouped by manufacturer brand to high priority at a very low bid, say $0.01 in an initial campaign – Call it Campaign A.

Then, I create another campaign set at either medium or low priority with the same product group set and use a significantly higher bid, say $1 – Call this Campaign B.

Within the high priority Campaign with bids set at $0.01 (Campaign A), I add negative keywords for the brand term as well as other high converting search terms.

What this does is allow Campaign A to filter out keyword searches with the use of negative keywords for $0.01. These are keywords that typically do not convert. Thus, this strategy allows only high converting traffic based on specific keywords to be eligible to serve product ads in Campaign B which greatly increases the conversion rates, CTR and overall profitability of Campaign B.

Now Campaign A, with its bid of $0.01 will still get a small bit of traffic and some of that traffic may even convert. When a keyword term converts in Campaign A, you can view the 'Search' terms report located within the 'Keywords' link on the left menu to add this keyword as a keyword negative to Campaign A. When you add a keyword negative to Campaign A, it will allow searches to be passed through to Campaign B.

This strategy works to greatly improve the conversion rates and particularly the CTR, which also increased the quality score of products ads in Campaign B. Increasing the quality score of products ads will work to benefit advertisers by helping lower their Average Cost-Per-Click regardless of bid. A product with a high-quality score often may be shown in front of a competitor's PLA ad regardless of bid, thereby increasing overall profitability even further!

Final Word

This is an advanced technique, and if you are somewhat new to using Google Shopping campaigns, you may need to read through the above example more than once for the strategy to make sense.

However, I promise that once you understand the Positive Keyword strategy fully explained in the next chapter and start to implement the strategy into your own campaigns, you will immediately reap the benefits when it comes to your overall profitability – return on ad spend (ROAS) numbers.

Note - this strategy is one of the first strategies I typically implement for new private clients in order to provide an immediate bump to profitability.

CHAPTER 24

Positive Keywords – A Better Way to Control Unwanted Searches

One of largest obstacles in achieving profitability for many advertisers using Google Shopping is the presence of unwanted keyword searches. Even profitable Shopping campaigns are not immune to wasted ad spend due to the nature of Google Shopping.

With Google Shopping, the advertiser, of course, does not select their keywords, which is different than with Search campaigns. Instead, Google uses their proprietary algorithm to match a user's Google search with an advertiser's product ad. In order to match an advertiser's product ad to serve inside Google Shopping results, Google uses a combination of keywords found in each product's title and its product description. Then Google uses a real-time auction based on an advertiser's bid compared with other advertisers' bids who have matching products to determine which order (ad rank) items appear in Google Shopping.

For the most part, this works well for advertisers as the keywords in the title and description determine when a product is eligible to appear, and the amount of an advertiser's bid determines the order.

It also saves time for advertisers. Once a data feed is approved in Google Merchant Center, products can begin running inside the Google Shopping platform within minutes.

In fact, it is so easy to launch a new Google Shopping campaign that it can be quite dangerous in terms of budget for the novice Google marketer.

For those advertisers wanting to optimize their campaigns for profit, the most effective tool in being able to eliminate unwanted searches is the proper use of negative keywords – see my article 'The Art of Adding Negative Keywords'.

Negative keywords can be applied at the ad group, campaign or multi-campaign level with the use of a negative keyword list. However, properly optimizing with negative keywords by using the search terms report can be a never-ending task of find and remove with the constant discovery of new unwanted search phrases.

A Better Way

For accounts that have products that are highly brand-oriented, there is an easier way to eliminate approximately 80% of unwanted search terms without the constant adding of negative keywords.

Interested?

It is called Positive Keywords.

One of the most effective strategies that I use for many of my private clients who are brand centric, this strategy relies on a couple of things:

1. The Proper Segmenting of Google Shopping Campaigns.

2. The Use of Priority Settings.

Properly Segmenting Google Shopping Campaigns

With best-practices, Google Shopping campaigns should be subdivided just like you do with Google Search Campaigns, meaning into a subset of like products. Since Google Shopping products rely on your data feed being supplied to Google Merchant Center, this is going to take some advanced planning and correctly implementing that plan when formatting your Merchant Center feed.

However, by properly segmenting your campaigns, advertisers will be able to more easily control unwanted searches with negative keywords as well as be able to better optimize bids for product ads based on historical data.

For additional information on optimizing product bids plus a FREE download, see my article 'Effectively Optimize Google Shopping Based on Your Past History, Nothing More'.

Properly Using Campaign Settings

When configuring a Google Shopping campaign, Google allows for the use of priority settings of high, medium and low. Priority settings, like the name implies, takes priority over bids in determining which product Google serves from an advertiser's account.

The priority settings kick-in if either the same product is in two different campaigns or if two different products in two different campaigns have a title/keywords that matches a Google search query.

Here is a quick written illustration:

Campaign A has a Priority Level of Low and contains product XYZ with a bid of $0.50.

Campaign B has a Priority Level of Medium and also contains product XYZ with a bid of $0.05.

Google is going to always display the product XYZ from Campaign B with the bid of $0.05 instead of from Campaign A even though the bid for the same product is 10X higher in Campaign A because of the priority level setting.

For detailed information on formatting your Priority Settings, read my article 'Knowing Your Priority Settings in Google Shopping'.

The Positive Keyword Strategy

Here is how the priority keyword strategy works:

I set a product group containing many related products typically products grouped by manufacturer brand to high priority at a very low bid, say $0.01 in an initial campaign – Call it Campaign A.

Then, I create another campaign containing the same products at either medium or low priority and use a significantly higher bid, say $1 – Call this Campaign B.

Within the high priority Campaign with bids set at $0.01 (Campaign A), I add negative keywords for the branded terms as well as other high converting search terms.

What this does is allow Campaign A to filter out keyword searches with the use of negative keywords at a bid of $0.01. The keyword searches that direct to Campaign A are typically keywords with a low chance of converting.

Thus, this strategy allows only high-converting, brand-specific traffic to be eligible to serve product ads in Campaign B. This greatly increases the conversion rates, CTR and overall profitability of Campaign B, allowing you to increase bids and increase your Search Impression Share.

Now Campaign A, with its bid of $0.01 will still get a small bit of traffic, and some of that traffic may even convert. When a keyword term converts in Campaign A, you can view the 'Search' terms report located within the 'Keywords' link on the left menu to add this keyword as a negative keyword to Campaign A. When you add a keyword negative to Campaign A, it will allow future searches for that converting keyword to be passed through to Campaign B.

This strategy works well to significantly improve the conversion rates and the CTR, which also will increase the quality score of products ads in Campaign B. Increasing the quality score of products ads will work to benefit advertisers by helping lower their average cost-per-click regardless of bid.

A product ad with a high-quality score often may be shown in front of a competitor's PLA ad in Google regardless of bid, thereby increasing overall profitability even further!

Non-Theoretical Example

One of my private clients sells T-shirts and hats, and one of their biggest selling brands is John Deere. For their John Deere Shopping campaign, we have found that keyword search terms containing John Deere convert while there are hundreds of other search terms that do not or at least do not profitably.

Therefore, by using the Positive Keyword strategy, we can filter out all keyword searches that do not contain John Deere from the John Deere Campaign.

> Campaign A – We will name 'Positive Strategy – John Deere' and add all John Deere product ads to this campaign with a bid of $0.01 and set the priority level to high. We will then add the negative keywords as a phrase match "John Deere".

> Campaign B – We will name 'John Deere – Standard' and add all John Deere product ads to this campaign with a bid of $0.50 and set the priority level to medium.

Since both campaigns have the same products all Google searches where these products would be eligible to appear will be sent to the

Positive Strategy – John Deere campaign unless those searches contain the keyword term "John Deere".

Positive Strategy – John Deere campaign has a bid of $0.01, which allows us to filter out all the unwanted keyword searches that we were receiving non-specific keyword searches from John Deere - Standard at the cost of $0.01 per click!

With the positive keyword strategy in place, John Deere – Standard will now receive traffic from search terms ONLY with the term John Deere in them, including terms such as 'John Deere Hat', 'John Deere Shirt', Etc.

See how it works!

Final Word

Using Positive Keywords is most effective when advertising brand centric products or with enough historical data for an advertiser to absolutely know which keyword search terms do and do not convert.

By using Positive Keywords, an advertiser needs to make sure they are not eliminating substantial traffic that has the potential to generate significant profitable sales.

In addition, advertisers need to make sure all steps are properly completed when setting their priority levels, bids and negative keywords. If there is an error in the way settings are configured, the Priority Keywords method will not have the desired results.

You also will want to monitor your Positive Keyword campaigns for conversions as you will want to add to negative keywords in the Positive Strategy campaign if the campaigns receive a conversion.

Finally, even after Priority Keyword method is running properly, it will still be necessary to monitor the keywords driving traffic and most likely continue to add negative keywords to your main campaign, just not as many:>

SECTION 6

Final Thoughts

Have you heard the fable about the Frog and the Scorpion? The story starts with a Frog sitting by a river and minding his own business when along comes a Scorpion.

The Scorpion walks up to the Frog. "Hello Mr. Frog," said the Scorpion. "I wonder if you might be so kind as to give me a ride across the river on your back."

Now the Frog knew that the Scorpion could not swim, but still he hesitated. "I don't think that's a good idea," said Frog. "You have a deadly sting, and you might kill me."

"But why would I do that?" replied the Scorpion. "If I stung you, we would both die."

The Frog thought about what the Scorpion said. "Okay, that makes sense. C'mon, Scorpion, jump onto my back and I will give you a ride across the river," the Frog said.

The Scorpion jumped onto Frog's back, and Frog began to swim across the river. But halfway across, Scorpion took his deadly stinger and stuck it into Frog's back

As the poison shot through the Frog, his body began to stiffen, and they both began to sink. "Why?" gasped Frog with his dying breath.

"Sorry, Frog," said Scorpion. "I had to do it, I'm a Scorpion." And Frog and Scorpion both died.

What Is A Small Business Scorpion?

Many small business owners (as frogs) face a scorpion all the time in the form of large Search Engine Marketing (S.E.M.) agencies.

Large S.E.M. agencies face an ongoing issue that is difficult to solve and that most of their clients don't even realize they have.

The larger an agency becomes, the more account executives they need to hire to optimize accounts for their clients. Quite often, the account executives they hire have little to no experience, and most of the time, they are lower paid positions, either employees right out of college or they are International, typically from India.

These junior account executives are quickly trained and then let loose to manage accounts, cutting their teeth learning as they go all on the client's ad spend. The larger an agency becomes, the more junior marketers they hire, repeating a nasty cycle that typically leads to poor results for their customers.

In addition, possibly even worse than turning over accounts (unbeknown to most clients) to a junior marketer with limited experience, is the fee structure that most search engine marketing companies use to determine what they charge clients.

Typically, clients are charged a percentage of how much they spend on online advertising through the agency. The going rate is between 15 and 20%.

Therefore, junior marketers controlling accounts and the agency they work for are heavily incentivized to spend as much of the client's money as possible, regardless of the results that they are producing.

Avoiding The Scorpion

In order not to be stung by a large S.E.M agency and their junior marketers that are set to handle your online advertising, you need to arm yourself.

Just like the frog wishes he had carried a stick, if you decide or have already turned over your advertising to a large S.E.M agency, you need to arm yourself with enough knowledge to know whether the S.E.M company you use is following best-practices, and if they are spending your advertising budget prudently.

By reading this book, you have taken the first step to avoid being the proverbial frog stung by the scorpion. In the final chapter, I will give you recommendations on where you can go to make sure you are never stung (at least as it pertains to Google Shopping!).

CHAPTER 25

Where Do You Go from Here?

As I put the final touches on this book working to dot the last 'i' and cross the last 't', the question inevitably will arise: where should you go from here?

Between the covers of the book (that you hopefully just read), you will find all the tools you need to successfully open your Google Merchant Center Account, link to your Google Ads account and successfully optimize your product listings based on historical data within your account.

Like I guaranteed in the beginning of this book, most likely by the time the book has been published and you have read it, some of the screenshots may be outdated (Google likes to move stuff around). However, the strategies and underlying fundamentals provided in this book will continue to perform well when properly applied.

For those of you running a business, you may not have the time to run your own Google Ads campaigns and may end up hiring an agency to run your Google Paid Ads.

That is okay. Many companies don't have the time or resources to manage their Google Ads and still manage to do well in terms of sales and profits.

However, the story I just shared of the of the frog and the scorpion underlines a major problem with completely turning over your online marketing to a large S.E.M (search engine marketing) agency.

That is why you need to make sure you know how to optimize your Google paid ads, and by reading this book, you have taken the first step.

For those of you who can dedicate their time to running their own Google campaigns, congratulations, with the knowledge you have in this book, you probably will be able to achieve better results than most agencies. After all, who is more concerned about you making a profit than YOU?!

Whether you decide to outsource or to handle Google advertising in-house, I invite you to stay up to date with the latest changes in one of two ways.

First, I encourage you to check out my blog at blog.trueonlinepresence.com. Here, you can quickly keep informed with the latest changes and strategies concerning online advertising and, specifically, Google advertising.

Second, I invite you to check out my private training academy - 'The Academy of Internet Marketing'.

Arming business owners with knowledge of how to be successful with their paid advertising is exactly why I launched The Academy of Internet Marketing.

A membership-training academy, The Academy of Internet Marketing is where I demonstrate techniques for those small to medium-sized businesses that I am unable to help as private clients due to my agency's policy of limiting the number of private clients.

Going beyond what I share in my blog, blog.trueonlinepresence.com, The Academy of Internet Marketing provides video courses on Google ads, Bing, Facebook, SEO and many other topics that are important to the success of an eCommerce business, including all of my new courses and *Google Shopping Simplified* that details many of the principles described in this book.

In addition to courses, The Academy of Internet Marketing has video tutorials and articles that detail both what is working as well as changes that occur in the world of internet marketing as well as exclusive access to me.

If you plan on running your advertising in-house, great. The Academy of Internet Marketing is a valuable resource to make sure that they are applying best practices to grow their Business while turning a healthy profit.

If you are using a large S.E.M. company, just as good. The Academy of Internet Marketing provides valuable insight so business owners can discover if their accounts are being handled properly.

Whether you are just starting your business, or you have been running an online business for decades, The Academy of Internet Marketing has transformed into the online marketing destination for those who are serious about substantially growing their online sales.

Today, The Academy of Internet Marketing (www.theacademyofinternetmarketing.com), is the premier online destination for small to mid-sized eCommerce businesses serious about substantially growing their online sales. Plus, exclusive access to me, author of *Make Each Click Count Using Google Shopping* Revealing Profits & Strategies and *Make Each Click Count, The TOP Guide To Success Using Google AdWords.*

If you have the dedication and are ready to take your online sales to the next level, then The Academy of Internet Marketing was created for you. It provides the tools in the form of knowledge of what works today.

If you are ready to take your online advertising to the next level, I welcome you to join us and see what makes us special, and together we will grow your business!

Happy Marketing!

Andy Splichal

MAKE EACH CLICK COUNT THE PODCAST

The Podcast that reveals new details in how to accelerate your sales and profits while making sure you are getting the absolute most from your marketing dollars!

Join Us Today And Start Making Each Click Count!

Available online through
Apple Podcast, Spotify and more. Or join us online at
www.makeeachclickcount.com/podcast